'Tom's ministry as an active ⌐ been complemented by that of hi⌐ ¬pton District Enabler for Me⁺¹ ₃es, they share thoughtful re ⌐ext of the Covid Pandemic. Th. ⌐ and letters, they offer encouragement ᴉ groups to perceive and experience the sustaining ᴗᴅ.'

Alison Judd, World Presia⌐.α 2016-2022 of the World Federation of Methodist and Uniting Church Women

'Tom Stuckey always writes with honesty and humanness. This is a book to stimulate in the here and now. Prophetic words are timeless! The message of *In and Out of Lockdown* speaks truth in an uncertain world and offers hope through personal reflection and imaginative Biblical exposition.'

Rev Dr. Richard Teal, Former President of the Methodist Conference

'Tom and Christine continue to offer their ministry through this powerful and challenging book. I was encouraged to reflect on my own response to the ongoing pandemic, enabled to find the voice of God through the noise of many distractions and further equipped in my own life and ministry. The Church is blessed by the wisdom and insights of Christine and Tom.'

Rev Andrew de Ville, Chair of the Methodist Southampton District

This is a fascinating follow-up to Tom Stuckey's previous angry book on Covid-19. Although new challenges invade our minds and disturb our lives, the pandemic is not over. Neither are its consequences. Our 'new normal' has become even more unstable than the old! Tom's collection of sermons and Bible studies encourages us to reflect on our own personal journey in and out of lockdown. Christine, Tom's wife, brings additional insight to this exploration as she charts her own spiritual journey through the pandemic.

How was your experience of lockdown? Did the sermons you heard bring illumination? Can studying the Old Testament book of Job empower us into a radically new normal? Jonah's dramatic journey in and out of lockdown taught him nothing. Why was this? What have we learnt? These are some of the questions raised by this publication.

The author believes that in reflecting, recognizing and coming to terms spiritually and theologically with Covid-19 and its consequences, can help us reshape our future with faith and hope.

This book offers exciting material to think about, study, discuss and pray over. This is the first of the author's Christchurch Collection. Will it be the last?

A Christchurch Collection

In and Out of Lockdown

TOM & CHRISTINE
STUCKEY

Foreword by Canon Charles Stewart

Dedication

Our Daughter Joanne Stuckey

BOOKS by TOM STUCKEY

COVID-19 GOD'S WAKE-UP CALL? Angry Bible Reflections in a Pandemic (2021).

METHODISM UNFINISHED; Studies based on the Reflections of Ten Methodists (2019).

THE WRATH OF GOD SATISFIED? Atonement in an Age of Violence (2012).

ON THE EDGE OF PENTECOST: A Theological Journey of Transformation (2007).

BEYOND THE BOX: Mission Challenges from John's Gospel (2005).

INTO THE FAR COUNTRY: A Theology of Mission for an Age of Violence (2003).

RAINBOW, JOURNEY AND FEAST: Biblical Covenants and a Theology of Mission (1988).

UNDERSTANDING OLD TESTAMENT PROPHETS TODAY; Bible Society (1985).

UNDERSTANDING NEW TESTAMENT LETTERS TODAY: Bible Society (1985).

CONTENTS

FOREWORD

We have it on Jesus' authority that we are to read the signs of the times. Rarely can that obligation have been more urgent than now. Lockdown may be a thing of the past, but Covid is still with us.

I came to *In and Out of Lockdown* fresh from reading Peter Hennessy's *A Duty of Care: Britain Before and After Covid* (Allen Lane, 2022). Where Lord Hennessy seeks to explore the state of the nation from an historical and political perspective, Tom Stuckey – with significant contributions from his wife, Christine – invites us instead to look at a number of crucial post-Covid questions from a position of Christian faith and practice. What are Christians to make of the experience of the pandemic? How can we ensure our 'new normal' does more than 'get back' to where we were before, but may be more fully aligned with the Kingdom of God?

From the Prologue onwards, Tom is clear-sighted in setting out the ground. So when he writes 'The new normal has become even less stable than the old', he backs up his claim (without ever scare-mongering) before going on to offer a hope-filled route into making sense of what we have been through, and how we might work together in God's future.

Part of this book's appeal is that we are drawn into these issues in different ways. Divided into five main sections, it contains three types of material. The first is a selection of sermons preached mainly in Christchurch Priory. It is good that others may now benefit from these sermons, in which Tom comes across as the thoughtful preacher, pastor and theologian the Priory congregation knows him to be. From Joseph's story comes encouragement: 'when your world falls apart, don't be afraid!' In 'Ministerial Madness', preached first to a gathering of Methodist ministers, we encounter a 'radically new perspective' that convinces both in its analysis and in its call, not for 'a restoration of the Church but a concentration on God's kingdom.' The prophetic message of this sermon is for every ecclesial community, including my own.

Two collections of letters – 'Lockdown Letters' and 'Letters of Liberation – form the second element in the book. Written by Christine Stuckey to Southampton District members of the Methodist Women in Britain team, these can helpfully be read alongside (in places, almost as a commentary) on Tom's sermons.

The third component of *In and Out of Lockdown*, and the most substantial, is material intended for small group use. In these two sets of studies, based respectively on the books of Job and Jonah, each session begins with Scripture, before going on to a thought-provoking reflection and finally offering some questions 'to ponder'. I commend these studies to any small group.

The public enquiry into Covid-19 has (finally) been launched: public hearings begin in Spring 2023. While its eventual report may get to the bottom of what happened, and why, and when, its Terms of Reference preclude any consideration of the issues raised by Tom Stuckey in *In and Out of Lockdown*. This timely book asks how we are to live now, with consideration for others; not looking for 'peace where there is no peace' (Jeremiah 6.14), but living in the peace that is God's promise to us all, as it was to Simeon; living with hope, affirming the place of truth in Christian thinking and action, and always confident that the light of Christ shines even in the darkest places. For all this, we may be grateful to Tom and Chris Stuckey for helping us read the signs of these times.

The Rev Canon Charles Stewart
Vicar of Christchurch Priory

PROLOGUE

Did Lockdown really happen? In Britain, Covid-19 is no longer newsworthy. Although other events now dominate the headlines, the effects and consequences of the pandemic still haunt us. According to a government-funded study, the number of people suffering from high levels of anxiety and depression, which soared by more than a third, 'are poised to remain with us for years to come'. [1] Not only are we facing a mental health crisis but there are over 1.4 million people with Long-Covid. In addition, there is a massive exodus of staff from hospitals and care homes because of illness, stress and low pay. Furthermore Covid-19 has left a legacy of anger, fear and uncertainty which is now being fed by several circumstances: the negative aspects of Brexit, Partygate, Russia's invasion of the Ukraine, the global fuel and food crisis, an increase in the cost of living at home, the possibility of new viruses and the ever-present climate challenge. The new normal has become even less stable than the old.

In my last book, [2] commenting on the need to actively address climate change, I concluded, 'If we do not respond quickly to this challenge we should not be surprised if something worse that the present pandemic suddenly shreds our "new normal" in order to bring us to our senses!' In Britain, neither nation nor Church has properly reflected on the lessons of Lockdown. I have written this book to encourage you to thoughtfully and prayerfully repeat that journey in and out of Lockdown. It is my hope that, this time around, you will discover those transformational insights which will equip you to face an uncertain future with confidence and hope.

Foreword and Prologue

There are two people I wish to thank: first, my wife Christine. Although she has consistently encouraged, commented and helped me in the writing of my previous books, this is the first time her own work has been published. Her material is included because it has reshaped my own thinking and also gives this book a much-needed personal perspective.

Secondly, I am also delighted that the Vicar of Christchurch Priory has agreed to write the Foreword. Charles Stewart has become a special friend. Our relationship began some eight years ago when, feeling spiritually lost and low, Christine and I turned up at the morning service. The worship and music were inspiring and the sermon thoughtful and challenging. Charles, who I had previously encountered at Winchester Cathedral when I was Chair of the Southampton Methodist District,[3] arranged to meet me for conversation and prayer. Although both Christine and I remain committed and active within the Methodist Church, Christchurch Priory is now my spiritual place of renewal. With gentle wisdom over the past few years, Charles has allowed me to preach occasionally and lead Bible Studies. This, my first 'Christchurch Collection', is my tribute to the Priory.

With most books you start at the beginning and work your way through. You can do the same here or you may wish to jump about. Parts 3 & 5 offer study material which is best worked at consistently in a group. In some respects these sections lie at the very heart of this publication and should be given extra attention. Parts 1, 2 & 4 can be used within your own personal devotion. Simply dip into these at random. You will find the concluding study of Jonah to be the climax of all that has gone before.

Foreword and Prologue

The few references in the writing can be tracked down in the Appendix. I wish to thank Les Judd and Nick Straw for giving attention to the text itself.

PART 1

SERMONS

In and Out of Lockdown

All of these sermons, apart from the last, were preached in the Christchurch Priory. Based on Lectionary Readings for the Sunday, they punctuate the period from September 2020 to October 2021 when we moved in and out of our second Lockdown.

All sermons have been slightly amended for this publication.

1

THE BIGGER PICTURE

Realizing that their father was dead, Joseph's brothers said, 'What if Joseph still bears a grudge against us and pays us back in full for all the wrong that we did to him?' So they approached Joseph, saying, 'Your father gave this instruction before he died, "Say to Joseph: I beg you, forgive the crime of your brothers and the wrong they did in harming you."'...

Joseph wept when they spoke to him. Then his brothers also wept, fell down before him, and said, 'We are here as your slaves.' But Joseph said to them, 'Do not be afraid! Am I in the place of God? Even though you intended to do harm to me, God intended it for good, in order to preserve a numerous people, as he is doing today. So have no fear...'

Genesis 50.15-21

It's wonderful to be back in church after the Spring lockdown when Christchurch Priory, along with every other Church in Britain, was closed for several months. Although worshipping on-line has fed us, not being able to meet physically, as we are doing today on September 13th, has been a real deprivation. I think we all felt relieved when Covid cases began to fall and restrictions were eased. It has been a difficult time. As I look around this morning, I note the absence of familiar faces. The pandemic has left a legacy of fear and loss.

Our current lectionary readings about Joseph and his brothers are reaching their conclusion. The continuing famine in

Canaan has forced the brothers to return again to Egypt. They are again given an audience with Pharaoh's deputy. Their last meeting had been traumatic. What will he demand of them this time round? They still do not recognise this powerful potentate to be the brother they had maligned, betrayed and sold off as a slave. When Joseph finally declares himself they are terrified. What's he going to do to them?

Turning to our Gospel reading in Matthew 18.23-34 we are also left wondering what's going to happen to the servant who owes his master a huge sum of money. This Matthew story demands a **financial** recompense. The Joseph story demands a **moral** recompense.

The servant in the Matthew story has to pay back 10,000 talents. It is an enormous sum. The total amount of tax collected by the Roman Authorities in the year 4BC from the whole of Judea, Israel and Palestine was 600 talents. This man owed 10,000 talents! We are talking of billions of pounds. It is not only over the top! It is ridiculous! What did he spend it on? The servant cannot lay his hands on such an incredible sum. What will the master do? Surprise, surprise! The master cancels the debt. This is generosity beyond one's imagination.

Joseph's brothers are also in an impossible situation. They quiver and quake; groveling before the person they have wronged. It is pay-back time! What will Joseph do? He addresses them, 'Don't be afraid! You did not sell me to this place, but rather God sent me here to preserve life'.

This is a story of God's saving and liberating providence at work for Joseph and his family. Because of their actions and the event of the famine (though the passage does not attribute the famine to God) a new beneficial future opens up for all of them.

Both stories remind us that however bad our situation there is bigger picture of generosity and grace. Our personal stories are part of a larger story about God's redeeming love. When your world falls to pieces, don't be afraid! When everything goes wrong, don't be afraid! When you feel crushed and unable to do anything; don't be afraid! Always remember there is a hidden providence at work which informs us that we must not regard ourselves as victims of events but rather as active shapers of the future. Your story will be swept up into God's story of freedom and grace. Even in a pandemic like Covid-19, God is going on ahead of us preparing humankind for a different and hopefully better tomorrow. Therefore, don't be afraid!

Jonathan Sacks writes, 'Joseph's life shows that we can defeat tragedy by our ability to see our life not just as a sequence of unfair events inflicted on us by others, but also as a series of divinely intended moves, each of which brings us closer to a situation in which we can do what God wants us to do.'[5]

In 2002 I was in South Africa on a lecture tour. After preaching in the main Methodist Church in Cape Town it was suggested that we go to Robyn Island. So on Monday morning, Chris and I waited at the Waterfront. It was bitterly cold and our small boat was shrouded in fog as we journeyed to the Island. What a desolate place it is. Our black guide, who was a cheerful chap, took us around. In one of the dormitories he paused and stood by a bed. 'That was my bed. I was teacher and I happened to complain about the treatment of the Bantu children. The police came by night. They seized me. They accused me of being a communist. They tortured me and imprisoned me here for 10 years.'

One from our group suddenly spoke up, 'How can you bear to return to this dreadful place?' His response stunned us. 'It was here in lockdown that I discovered forgiveness and freedom. When the guards brutalized us they were destroying their own humanity and this allowed us to discover ours. We were free! They were the ones imprisoned'

In the silence which followed we were no longer tourists. We felt ourselves to be pilgrims gazing into a new future. The clinging fog was still there on our return boat trip, but as we entered Cape Town harbour the sun suddenly broke through and shone upon us with freedom light.

There is a better story and a bigger picture. It is about hope. Hope for you, for me and for all humanity. So don't be afraid!

SOMETHING TO THINK ABOUT
There was a saving providence at work in Jacob's dysfunctional family. The famine disaster was a key event opening up a new future. In our dysfunctional world can we detect a similar gracious providence at work in and through Covid-19?

2

THE ANNUCIATION

The angel said to her, 'Do not be afraid, Mary, for you have found favour with God. And now, you will conceive in your womb and bear a son, and you will name him Jesus. He will be great, and will be called the Son of the Most High...'

Mary said to the angel, 'How can this be, since I am a virgin?'

The angel said to her, 'The Holy Spirit will come upon you, and the power of the Most High will overshadow you...'

Then Mary said, 'Here am I, the servant of the Lord; let it be with me according to your word.'

Luke 1. 30-38

Four years ago Justin Welby in his Christmas sermon spoke of the economics of despair and of how our world had 'become awash with fear and division.' There are over 365 references to fear in the Bible; fear of death, fear of failure, fear of loss, fear of disaster, fear of the enemy and fear of the unknown. Now with the arrival from India of a new more virulent Covid variant, fear has again been reawakened in many senior citizens.

Zechariah is terrified when an angel suddenly stands beside him in the temple. The shepherds on the hillsides of Bethlehem are scared witless when a heavenly messenger arrives in the middle of the night. When the angel Gabriel appeared before Mary she is described as being 'much perplexed'. This is a feeble translation of her reaction. She was more than confused; she was petrified with fear. The angel's response is also strong. 'Don't let more fears pile on top of your fear' (The meaning of the Greek word *diatarasso*).

Most of the Bible references to fear occur in the Old Testament – nearly 300 of them. The 'Do not be afraid' message saturates the book of Isaiah: 'Do not be afraid. I am with you' (41.10); 'Do not be afraid. I will help you' (41.14); 'Do not be afraid. I have redeemed you.' (43.1). Chapter 7 describes panic in the besieged city of Jerusalem as they fear an attack from their Northern neighbours. How does the prophet address their fears? He declares, 'Behold a virgin shall conceive and bear a son and his name shall be called Emmanuel – God is with us!' The word Isaiah uses for 'virgin' is literally 'a young woman'. Does this mean there is no virgin birth? Not at all! John in his Gospel announces that Jesus was born 'not of blood, nor of flesh, nor by the will of a husband, but of God' (1.13). That ancient promise is realised in Mary. 'Can it be true?' she asks. It is true!

Are all promises true? 'I will make America great', says Donald Trump. Can it be true? 'We will be much better off after Brexit'. Will we? 'We have a world-beating track and trace system,' says our Prime Minister. Do we? 'What is truth?' is the age-old question asked by Pilate.

Matthew D'Ancona, in his 2017 book entitled *Post-Truth*, describes how the re-wiring of the world through social media and web-enabled cell phones has changed the nature of democracy by fuelling a culture where feelings rather than facts reshape our understanding of truth. We digest the news which makes us feel good and which reinforces our fantasies. In today's world of smoke and mirrors, 'news' is often Government propaganda and not something factually determined. So what is truth?

'How can it be?' asks Mary. 'Give me some factual explanation.' The angel's response is to tell her about her cousin Elizabeth who, in old age, has become pregnant. This would have reminded Mary of those Old Testament miracle stories of Sarah giving birth to Isaac, Hannah giving birth to Samuel and Manoah's wife producing Sampson. Can it be true? YES it can!

How did she prove it? She goes to Elizabeth to test out Gabriel's promise. The shepherds on the hillside hear the angelic message. 'Do not be afraid for today in the city of David a Saviour has been born. Here is the sign. You will find the baby wrapped in cloths and lying in a manger.' How did they prove it? They go to Bethlehem and check it out.'

Mary's response is so different than Zechariah's. 'How will I know?'. He gets the answer he deserves. 'Because you did not believe my words you will not be able to speak when you leave this place. Mary's is not the egocentric question, 'How will I know?' but an open question, 'How can this be?' And her response! LET IT BE! Let it be to me according to your word.

How can this be for me? You must open up your heart, mind and soul, just as Mary did, and let Jesus in.

O Holy Child of Bethlehem, descend to us we pray,
Cast out our sin and enter in, be born in us today!

SOMETHING TO THINK ABOUT
How does one tell the difference between 'fake news' and 'news' which is honest and true?

14

3

CANDLEMAS

'Master, now you are dismissing your servant in peace, according to your word; for my eyes have seen your salvation, which you have prepared in the presence of all peoples, a light for revelation to the Gentiles and for glory to your people Israel.'

Luke 2.29-32

The easing of restrictions over Christmas and the subsequent arrival of a new variant has produced a Covid surge with over 1,000 deaths each day. Once again we are back in lockdown and this sermon is being preached 'online'.

We have not been able to meet up with our children and grandchildren for several months so our family Christmas celebrations have been postponed. Some years ago I was visiting a housebound member of my congregation in Bristol. It was Holy Week and the Christmas decorations were still up. I commented on this. Had Christmas been postponed? 'No. It's because my husband is too lazy to take the trimmings down'.

Traditionally the decorations should come down on Twelfth Night to herald the feast of Epiphany with the coming of the wise men. Epiphany is the season of light culminating in Candlemas which we celebrate on Tuesday, forty days after Christmas Day. It takes us halfway through the winter. We look back at the incarnation and forward to the passion of Christ. It is still about light - not one small flickering candle - but an accumulation of light which drives away the darkness. In days gone by on the feast of Candlemas, people came to church bringing candles to be lit. The congregation would then return to their homes carrying with them the light of Christ.

Our Prime Minister talks of light at the end of the tunnel because of the discovery of a vaccine. I'm talking about light **in** the tunnel because of Christ. Here is light of such intensity that no darkness can quench it; light of such luminosity that tunnels are no more. This is God's laser light piercing every dark corner of the world. In the words of Simeon, 'It is a light for revelation to the Gentiles and for glory to your people Israel'. Simeon beheld it in the baby Jesus.

Shepherds, representing ordinary everyday people, came to the manger. Magi from the East representing the rich, wise and learned also arrived. Today's Gospel lesson tells of two old people – Simeon and Anna – who had awaited this moment for years.

I have yet to celebrate my eightieth birthday which occurred last May. When you pass your three-score-years and ten, what do you anticipate? Richard Holloway, a former bishop of Edinburgh, in his recent book writes;

Reading obituaries encourages me to confess my own condition. I take my place in the wide circle in the waiting room and say to the others assembled, 'Good evening. My name is Richard, and I suffer from a terminal disease called mortality. Like all of you in here tonight, I am waiting for the last bus.'[6]

The frightening daily death toll of those who have died from Covid-19 reminds all of us of our mortality. Hundreds of thousands in Britain are being forced to think about death. Simeon, like Richard

Holloway, is another person who contemplates his own death and does so with equanimity and joy. He praises God and exclaims, 'Lord, let your servant depart in peace for my eyes have seen your salvation!'

What had prepared him for this last adventure? We have a number of clues. First, we are told he was righteous and devout and looked for the consolation of Israel. He was not self obsessed or caught up in his own agenda, too busy to think about wider issues. He directed his gaze outwards, thinking of others and praying for their welfare. Second, the Holy Spirit rested on him. He knew that one day the light he had been waiting for would illuminate his heart and soul.

Marjorie Wheeler attended worship at my church in Reading. She was eighty-seven. We used to hold music evenings in the manse during Lent. It was Holy Week and twelve of us met to listen to parts of J.S.Bach's *St Matthew's Passion*. She was brought to this event by a member of our congregation. She phoned me the next day. 'I was brought to Sunday School by my parents and have been a regular worshipper here at Wesley Church ever since. I have heard people speak of experiencing Jesus, but it has never happened to me. As I listened to the music last night, great waves of peace washed over me. I felt bathed in light. At long last near the end of my life I have truly experienced God's salvation'.

SOMETHING TO THINK ABOUT
You can find the peace and purpose you are looking for. It has been promised.

4

PRUNING AND GROWING

> *'I am the true vine, and my Father is the vine-grower. He removes every branch in me that bears no fruit. Every branch that bears fruit he prunes to make it bear more fruit...Those who abide in me and I in them bear much fruit, because apart from me you can do nothing.'*

> John 15.1-5

'I am the true vine and my father is the vine-grower'. That's the Bible text. At home we have another arrangement. 'I am the grass cutter and my wife is the gardener'. I do not have green fingers, however when we were moved to Chandlers Ford my study window looked out at a vine attached to a sunny wall. For the first year I watched its abundant growth but was disappointed by the lack of grapes. I sought advice. A friend, who knew about these things, arrived in the autumn. Talk about cutting back! There was hardly anything left by the time he had finished. He taught me how to prune. I had never realised how drastic this process had to be: reducing the number of growing bunches in May; removing excess growth to give more ventilation in the summer; then the fiddly job of thinning each bunch. It was time consuming yet relaxing. It was an escape from Church! But, no, it is the Church.

If the Church is to experience Pentecost and be filled with the new life of the Spirit two things are necessary: FIRST a pruning or cutting back and SECOND a planting of the Holy Spirit in our hearts so that we can abide in Christ and bear fruit.

The Covid-19 lockdowns led many of us to engage in a home pruning process. Lofts and garages have been cleaned out; useful stuff taken to charity shops; accumulated junk to the rubbish tip. Today's reading tells us that the unfruitful branches are to be burnt. But what of the good growing parts that have been chopped back to produce a better grape? The lockdowns have deprived us of many good things: meeting friends, going out, worshiping in church and singing hymns. If we view this as a pruning process, what has it taught us?

The coronavirus has certainly provoked questions about equality, fairness and togetherness. Indeed, 'the present crisis has revealed our vulnerability and exposed the false securities on which we base our lives'.[7] The 126,000 deaths in Britain remind us of our mortality. The harrowing pictures of what is happening in other parts of the world trumpet the fragility and unfairness of life.

> Thy world is weary of its pain,
> Of selfish greed and fruitless gain,
>
> Look down on all earth's sin and strife,
> And lift us to a nobler life.

This prayerful dream of hope by John H.B. Masterman, Bishop of Plymouth, written after the First World War, is as relevant today as it was one hundred years ago.

The farewell chapters 13-17 in John's Gospel from which today's lesson is taken contain the Covid themes of loss, death, saying good-bye, anxiety about the future, shattered plans, disappointed hopes and a painful exposure to reality. Jesus is taking his disciples from their old normal and pointing them to a new creation! Covid-19 can be viewed as God's wake-up call: a challenge to root out the material, emotional and spiritual baggage which clog up our hearts and minds and to seek a better future of justice and peace for all people. We have been pruned, cut back, emptied out. What next?

With the gradual lifting of lockdown restrictions, Christine and I were able at the beginning of May to visit our favourite eating place in Christchurch for breakfast and coffee - in proper mugs rather than paper cups. It was wonderful! It was normal. We all want to get back to normal. But wait! Should we not first pause and reassess? How are we going to re-fill the empty spaces that have been created because of Covid?

The farewell chapters in John's Gospel make the disciples fearful and anxious as Jesus prepares his disciples for his imminent death. However, alongside his final 'good-byes' is a big 'hello' to the Comforter - the Holy Spirit. This promised Spirit will be our Advocate (14.15). He will teach us, equip us and fill us with peace and power (14.25). He will make Jesus real for you and for others (15.26). He will put things right (16.7). When we allow the Holy Spirit to dwell in us, unexpected doors will open, new opportunities will arise and a different future will unfold.

> Pruning and Growing.
> Emptying and Filling!

Today's other New Testament reading for 6th May is part of Acts 8. It describes what happened when the Holy Spirit came upon Philip, one of the newly appointed deacons in the early Church. Philip was in charge of the food-bank in Jerusalem when the Holy Spirit grabbed him. He was whisked off to explain the Bible to the Ethiopian Chancellor of the Exchequer who just happened to be whizzing by in his chariot. Phillip hitched a lift. He spoke of Jesus.

They stopped for a baptism before Philip was again snatched away and sent off to a distant place. It's fast moving stuff. The story ends with joy, rejoicing and fruitfulness.

We are not meant to go back and do what we did before. A pruning and an emptying process has taken place. A Holy Spirit filling is now required.

'

**Let the Spirit fill you, so that you can dwell in Christ
and so that Christ can live in you.
Amen**

SOMETHING TO THINK ABOUT
How has your value system changed because of lockdown?

5

LOOK AT THE NATURAL WORLD

'Therefore I tell you, do not worry about your life, what you shall eat, what you shall drink or what you shall wear...Look at the birds of the air; they neither sow nor reap nor gather into barns, and yet your heavenly Father feeds them.'

Matt.6.26f

We are being told not to panic because of fuel and food shortages. This exhortation seems to be having the opposite effect on people. The instructions of Jesus, in the Sermon on the Mount, provide an antidote to worry and panic. Today he could be saying, 'Don't worry if some of the shelves in the supermarket are empty or if petrol stations have run out of fuel, or there is a shortage of turkeys; look beyond these consumer wants to the natural world. If you carefully observe the flowers and the birds you will learn some important lessons'.

Alas our heavenly Father does not appear to feed the birds where we live. I am always filling up our bird feeder. The blue tits, great tits and finches have enormous appetites. Jesus tells us to look at the birds of the air. I do! I have now given up chasing off the rooks that descend in battalions on our front lawn and hack it to pieces. Things don't seem to be quite as straightforward as Jesus suggests.

We had a wonderful reading today from the Old Testament book of Joel. 'O children of Zion, be glad and rejoice in the Lord your God; he has poured down abundant rain...The threshing-floors shall be full of grain...You shall eat in plenty and be satisfied, and praise the name of the Lord your God'. The prophet is promising an abundant harvest! If we had read from chapter one, however, we would have heard how the country had been devastated by plagues of locusts.

The Covid pandemic was not the only disaster of 2020. A second plague of locusts was at the same time devastating the countries of the Middle East and Africa. The first wave had begun in 2018 when a voracious breed swarmed across the regions of the Gulf. These locusts could eat as much food in a day as could be consumed by 35,000 people.

Jesus is right when he tell us that our natural world can be a great source of renewal and delight. Many of us discovered this during lockdown. There is, however, a shadow side. St Paul, in Romans 8, speaks of creation groaning in pain and agony because it has been subjected to futility. Commentators tell us that the word 'futility' suggests our universe is in pain because it is being subjected to the rampant activities of human beings who plunder and rape the earth. Our natural world is not as it should be. Things are out of joint. We are largely responsible.

In his popular book The *Revenge of Gaia,* James Lovelock dared to suggest that if we fail to be responsible, the earth will take care of itself by making us no longer welcome. I note that during the pandemic the rate of polluting gases dropped by nearly 50%. While Covid 19 was bad news for the money men, it was good news for the planet. Is the planet starting to strike back at us? It makes you wonder! What new disaster is going to overtake us next?

The World Climate Change Conference is to be held in Glasgow at the beginning of November. What will be the outcome? The Kyoto Protocol seeking the stabilisation of greenhouse gas emissions came into force in February 2005. Not all the rich polluting nations signed up to it. Moreover, most of those who did have not implemented the key proposals, and that includes the UK. It has been words rather than actions up until now. Will things be any different this time? There are indications that China and India (two of the world's biggest polluters) may not be attending.

Jesus in our text is speaking about worry and the natural world. I am not worried for myself, but I do worry about my grandchildren. Is there an antidote to worry? Jesus says, '**Look at** the birds and **consider** the lilies of the field'. The same Greek word *emblepo* is used in both cases. The usual word 'to look' is *blepo*. Here the word is *emblepo*. This form of the word is telling us to 'really look'; 'to look straight at it', 'to look into it'. Put everything you have into the looking until you are one with what you are observing and start to see what you have not seen before. Artists and scientists know something of this.

FIRST, in looking we see evidence of God's goodness and loving kindness.

> Said the robin to the sparrow; 'I should really like to know
> Why these anxious human being rush about and worry so'.
> Said the sparrow to the robin: 'Friend, I think that it must be
> That they have no heavenly Father, such as cares for you and
> me.'[8]

When you really 'Look at the birds of the air and consider the lilies of the field' – you will open yourself up to the possibility of renewal and joy. Jesus therefore exhorts us to TRUST. In the words of the Pratt Green hymn we have just sung:

For the fruits of all creation, thanks be to God.

For the gifts to every nation, thanks be to God.
For the wonders that astound us,
for the truths that still confound us,
Most of all that love has found us, thanks be to God.

SECOND, in looking we see evidence of how we are destroying the planet. Pratt Green, in another of his hymns, presents us with this shadow side:

The earth is the Lord's: it is ours to enjoy it,
Ours, as God's stewards, to farm and defend.
From its pollution, misuse and destruction,
Good Lord, deliver us, world without end!

The Protestant Reformer Martin Luther commenting on our text says, 'Jesus is making the birds our teachers. It is an abiding disgrace that the little sparrow should be wiser than our teachers and our leaders'.

The Sermon on the Mount ends with the story of a wise man and a foolish man. One builds his life on sand and the other on rock. The wise man is the one who hears the words of Jesus and obeys them. So must we.

SOMETHING TO THINK ABOUT
Covid-19 was good for the planet. If we do not respond positively to the climate challenge, what new disaster might overtake us?

6

MINISTERIAL MADNESS

Then there came a voice to him that said, 'What are you doing here, Elijah?' He answered, 'I have been very zealous for the LORD, the God of hosts; for the Israelites have forsaken your covenant, thrown down your altars, and killed your prophets with the sword. I alone am left, and they are seeking my life, to take it away.' Then the LORD said to him, 'Go, return on your way to the wilderness of Damascus; when you arrive, you shall anoint Hazael as king over Aram. Also you shall anoint Jehu son of Nimshi as king over Israel; and you shall anoint Elisha son of Shaphat of Abel-meholah as prophet in your place... Yet I will leave seven thousand in Israel, all the knees that have not bowed to Baal, and every mouth that has not kissed him.'

1 Kings 19.13-18

It's a terrifying privilege to preach to a congregation of ordained ministers and priests. All of you, at some time or other, will have preached on Elijah and the still small voice. Reading this story recently I noted, in chapters 18 & 19, three major periods of ministry: the normal, the abnormal and the new normal. Normal ministry with its spectacular deeds ended at Carmel. Elijah goes into lockdown where God challenges him, 'What are you doing here?' The Spirit was attempting to prepare him for a radically different ministry.

First. What of the old normal?

PART 1 *Sermons*

Chapter 18 gives an account of a busy day. It began with preaching. 'How long will you hop about from one leg to the other?' (v.21). Not a promising text! Then comes an extraordinary half-day meeting with Ahab and 450 crazy prophets. Next there is a property matter - repairing a ruined altar (v.32). This is followed by some blood sports; first with a bull and then with his priestly opponents. Next he climbs a mountain but God is now slow in answering his prayer. When the rain finally comes Elijah runs 17 miles to Jezreel, even overtaking Ahab's chariot on the way which had left some time before. It was indeed a busy day. What next? He had a nervous breakdown: the fear, the flight, the abandoning of companions, the lack of appetite, paranoia and pathetic self-pity.

Many of us, like Elijah, are trapped in a form of ministerial madness as we attempt to keep the church going: initiating new ventures, caring for aging congregations, preaching, teaching, business meetings, responding to community needs, dealing with conflict, being available 24/7. Much of our sense of weariness does not arise from personal inadequacy but from what has been termed 'structural stressing' - something caused by the church organization itself. It increases dramatically in a declining church. Thus we are dragged from ministering to managing. We cease to be prophets and become process engineers. Do we really want to return to that? Many loyal hard working lay members, priests and ministers are starting to say with Elijah, 'It is enough!'

Second. What of the abnormal?

Surveys of the congregations in our area have shown that the majority of congregations (nearly all of them elderly) want to go back to church and do what they did before. We members of the ordained clergy may soon be caught up in a game of 'catch up'. In the rush to return to 'normal business' we can easily neglect the necessity of prayerfully articulating and learning from our shared experience of spiritual disorientation and the loss. This is not missing in the Elijah story; indeed, it is the essential element in the reshaping of his future ministry.

At the heart of my last book,[2] there is a chapter entitled 'lament'. Following Walter Brueggemann and others I have argued that we cannot move from the old to the new without the exercise of lament. Lament has several ingredients. There is grief which needs to be expressed. There is depression and fear. There is anger which needs to be vented. There is personal accountability which needs to be acknowledged. There is memory which can inspire possibility. These elements are all present in the whining words of Elijah as God attempts to re-orientate his perspective with the question, 'What are you doing here?'

The drama of God's redemption in Christ takes place over three days and yet we rush from Good Friday to Easter Day. Alan Lewis, in his monumental book on Holy Saturday writes of how we discover new truth by waiting between the old and the new and staring into the abyss because 'beyond the void, out of nothing, comes a new existence where despair makes way for joy.'[9]

Third. What of the new normal?

Lessons learnt during Lockdown.
- We have discovered ways of working which have by-passed church buildings.
- We have discovered ways of conferencing, meeting and enjoying fellowship without having to travel.
- We have discovered people, who previously did not attend church, tuning into our online service.

This is encouraging. But hold on a minute? Does this mean that we go back to doing what we did before but tweak our activities to take account of the new lessons?

Elijah was told to do something radically different, something he had **not** done before. 'Anoint Hazael, appoint Jehu and get Elisha to do what you were doing. Then a remarkable disclosure! 'There are a lot of new people out there of whom you are unaware. They will be the future people of God'. Sadly several chapters later, Elijah forgets this new still small voice perspective and falls back into his former crazy pattern of a wind and fire ministry.

CONCLUSION

What am I suggesting? A radically new perspective! We must not return to maintaining the **church** as it was, but are called to focus on the **world** as it ought to be. Decentralization, dispersion, fewer buildings, inspirational worship, theological depth, working for justice, seeking secular partners: these are the watchwords for the future. Covid-19 has come as God's wake-up call demanding a total re-orientation of our Church life so that we are properly prepared for a very uncertain future and ready to face sudden and unexpected challenges. We should not be surprised if something worse than the present pandemic shreds our 'new normal'!

What are you doing here Elijah? I want to get back to doing what I did before. NO!

The agenda has changed. Not a restoration of the Church but a concentration on God's kingdom.

SOMETHING TO THINK ABOUT
What are we doing here?

PART 2

LOCKDOWN LETTERS

This selection of letters charts the descent into lockdown. Christine began writing these to committee members of the Southampton District *Methodist Women in Britain* team. MWiB is part of an international Methodist organisation of faith, compassion and hope. The aim is to encourage women everywhere to develop a creative Christian spirituality which engages in practical social action in a multitude of global contexts.

With the advent of Lockdown, the letters served not only to keep the group together but to inform and raise morale. Only some of the weekly letters are included here and these have been suitably edited for a wider audience.

These letters cover the lockdown period from April 2nd – 26th June 2020. They are reproduced as written, save for minor amendments to punctuation.

2nd APRIL 2020

So here we are at last in Lockdown. Life has suddenly become very restricted. We are no longer able to go out when we want; only essential shopping; having to order food on-line; no public transport; no getting in the car; no corporate worship; locked church buildings; not having the freedom to meet with friends and, above all, prevented from seeing our three children and four grandchildren - all of whom live many miles away. It's so isolating. To cope with this, I am attempting to develop a rhythm to my days. It's not easy and I get very down at times. I am training myself to see this enforced isolation as a gift. Instead of rushing around and not having time to do things properly I am trying to slow up and concentrate much more on the job in hand and leaving other things for another day.

I have set myself to read more and work on the piece of sewing I have had for ages (It may even get finished!!). Music has always been important for Tom and I so we are listening to new pieces as well as music we have not heard for a long time. I have returned to playing the piano regularly.

Our daily exercise, either walking or cycling is a wonderful release, especially with the good weather we have been enjoying.

We tune-in most days to the streamed Daily Prayer from Christchurch Priory. There are nearly 30 of us. We are now on the readers' list. We also join with others in showing our appreciation for the NHS staff on Thursday evenings at 8pm with our 'doorstep clap'. Most people in our street come out to do this and we wave to each other. This event decreases our sense of isolation and makes us again feel part of our community.

I found this quote by St. Teresa of Avila (1515-1582)

> *Let nothing disturb you, Let nothing make you afraid. All things are passing,*

God alone never changes (in his love and care for you)
Patience gains all things.
If you have God you will want for nothing, he alone
suffices.

Love, peace & blessing, Chris.

9th APRIL 2020

What wonderful weather we are having at the moment. Enjoying the beauty of nature, the spring flowers and hearing the birds, makes us forget about what is happening within our own country and in other parts of the world.

The large number of deaths in hospitals and care homes and the news of those around us contracting Covid 19 sometimes overwhelms me, yet there are also signs of hope. The dedication of NHS staff, the response of 750,000 who have volunteered to work for the NHS, the clapping on Thursdays at 8pm and stories of kindness and care being demonstrated by neighbours; these are reminders of the resilience of the human spirit and a determination to work for good.

I'm sure, like me, you get anxious for your families and long for the time when we can meet up again. When I think about the events of Maundy Thursday, Good Friday and Easter Sunday, I tell myself to rejoice in Jesus' triumph over death. Julian of Norwich lived through the fears of the Black Death which swept the country in the 14th century. She held onto three truths revealed to her: God made us; God loves us; God sustains us. This enabled her to affirm:

All shall be well and all manner of things shall be well.

God's Spirit of love is moving through the universe. This love will hold us fast and never let us go.

Love, peace & blessing, Chris.

16th APRIL 2020

Christ is Risen. Alleluia!! I hope you were able to celebrate Easter through streamed services, radio or local church arrangements.   Tom & I tuned in to the Easter Morning Eucharist from Christchurch Priory. It was conducted from various homes. John's account of Mary's meeting with Jesus in the garden was read in a garden. Suddenly a blackbird started to sing. The message of resurrection was unexpectedly being serenaded by a blackbird in full song! It was most wonderful!

I have been enjoying my daily exercise. I have walked several times to a beautiful oak tree nearby. Those of you who came on one of the Pilgrimages I led, may remember that we stopped there to reflect and pray. When I visited the tree at the beginning of the lockdown there were just small buds on the branches. Now, after just a few weeks, the leaves are open. Nature with its returning life reminds me of God's promise of hope. When I open my eyes and really look I keep discovering God Moments to celebrate even when I struggle, feel downhearted or depressed.

In the darkness of sorrow let me glimpse joy;
in the darkness of suffering let me find comfort;
in the darkness of despair let hope suddenly appear.
Remind me that darkness cannot quench the light,
and that Jesus is the true light who will illuminate the
world. Amen.

Love, peace & blessing, Chris.

23rd APRIL 2020

Another week in Lockdown. It looks as if there will be many more. The glorious weather is a blessing. I can get out for exercise, work in the garden and get on with things which need to be done in the house. I do have times when I feel very frustrated at not being able to meet up with family, go out with Tom for coffee, work at the cafe in St. George's Church in Boscombe, enjoy the company of friends and do all the things I want to do with other people.

I have been attempting to learn the easy parts of some of Beethoven's Piano Sonatas. I find his music so captivating and inspirational. I marvel that, although he knew terrible isolation because of his deafness, he was able to transcend his frustration with music which communicated joy.

The gospel reading on Sunday was John 20.19-30. It struck me, as never before, that those disciples were in Lockdown! They too were behind shut doors, afraid, bewildered, upset and unsure of the future. Yet Jesus came and said 'Peace be with you'. He said it three times. I imagine him doing the same thing right now. He will keep saying it until we get it.

> *In the mist the sun breaks through;*
>
> *Beyond the dark clouds of night, stars illuminate the sky;*
>
> *In our troubled lives, the love of Christ enfolds us;*
>
> *In a world of unrest, pain and suffering, Jesus comes and says 'Peace'.*

Love, peace & blessing, Chris.

30ᵗʰ APRIL 2020

When I switched on the news today expecting doom and gloom, I was pleasantly surprised. It was all about Captain Tom's birthday, the incredible amount of money raised through his daily walk and the amazing flypast by Spitfire and Hurricane aircraft! What an inspiration he has become; so unassuming yet what he achieved went beyond his wildest dreams.

There is always good news if we look for it. A lot of people do recover from Covid-19 even though these figures are not published. For the past two Thursdays we have clapped our bin men. Most of our neighbours have staggered from their beds to stand on their doorsteps at 7am to wave, cheer and clap. The bin men looked so pleased to be acknowledged in this way. It was such a simple thing to do. Are we learning to give thanks for those forgotten workers who enable us to live comfortably? Will such thanksgiving last beyond the pandemic?

On Sunday I heard a sermon on Luke 24 - the story of the two disciples on the Emmaus Road. It's a favourite passage of mine. They were depressed, devastated and bewildered by a recent event in Jerusalem. We are only told the name of one of them – Cleopas. Was the other person his wife or could the other one be you? Or me? Imagine yourself there. An unknown stranger joins them. They walk and talk together and wonderful things start to happen. He listens, explains, is invited into their home and breaks bread. It is the Lord! Christ is Risen, Alleluia!!

> *Loving God, open our eyes to see the good things*
> *around us.*
> *Tune us in to the song of the birds and the beauty of*
> *nature.*
> *Teach us to be grateful for the people who have inspired*
> *us to reach beyond ourselves and achieve great things.*
> *As we walk each day with you, may we enjoy*
> *the wonder of living in the light of the risen Christ.*
> *Amen.*

Love, peace & blessing, Chris.

7th MAY 2020

Another beautiful morning! I can't help thinking that this Lockdown has been made bearable for me because of the sparkling sunny weather. It must be so hard for those living in cramped rooms, in tower blocks with no access to gardens or green spaces. How blessed we are to be living in such a lovely area.

Our country is in rather a muddle. It feels as if we are trying to walk through treacle. Over the past weeks I have become aware of how a spirit of fear is starting to stalk our nation. Fear is somehow being instilled or awakened in us. Outgoing people I know are afraid to leave their homes or go to a shop. We start to view the stranger with suspicion. Above all there is the unspoken fear of death. Should our actions be motivated by fear? Fear distorts and paralyses.

This week I read about Martin Rinkart. He was an Evangelical German Pastor during the Thirty Years War (1618-1648) and wrote the hymn, 'Now Thank We All Our God'. He used it as a grace before family meals. At the same time as this tragic war was raging, his country was being devastated by a terrible pestilence (their equivalent to Covid-19). It decimated the population. Martin presided over many deaths, including that of his wife who was one of its victims. Yet this hymn, which we have all sung many times, reflects no anger or despair in the face of suffering and loss, but rather joy and gratitude. God holds us in his arms and blesses us on our way. The hymn celebrates the 'wondrous things' done by 'this bounteous God'. It invites us to trust in God's goodness and grace because He 'frees us of all ills' and fills us with hope. Let this hymn be your prayer right now!

> *Now thank we all our God*
> *with hearts and hands and voices,*
> *who wondrous things has done,*
> *in whom this world rejoices;*

PART 2 Lockdown Letters

who, from our mother's arms,
has blessed us on our way
with countless gifts of love,
and still is ours today.

O may this bounteous God
through all our life be near us,
with ever joyful hearts
and blessed peace to cheer us;
and keep us in God's grace,
and guide us when perplexed,
and free us from all ills,
in this world and the next.

Love, peace & blessing, Chris.

14th MAY 2020

It was a sunny Friday in our street when we held our socially distanced street party to commemorate VE Day. It was amazing. Almost everyone had responded: houses decorated with bunting, chairs and tables placed on front lawns, drinks and nibbles. We had become a community experiencing release and freedom even when adhering to the two metre rule. There must have been over fifty of us spilling out from our lawns onto a road devoid of traffic. We were finding a brief moment of release from lockdown: smiling, shouting, cheering and talking - fortified by food and drink. I had conversations with neighbours I had not spoken to before. New friendships were being forged. The Queen, in her address later that day, spoke of the love which exists in our streets and communities.

The celebrations continued on Sunday when Tom joined the ranks of octogenarians! As all our family celebrations had to be cancelled, we held a family zoom time. I had, unknown to Tom, arranged for the people in our street - our neighbours - to stand in the road outside our bungalow at midday and sing 'Happy Birthday'. The doorbell rang. I told Tom to answer it.

He could not believe his eyes when he opened the door. There they were nearly thirty people, young and old, gathered in the road singing for him! He afterwards, with tears in his eyes, said it was the most surprising celebration he had ever had.

The Christian life is about 'fasting and feasting'; about 'wilderness and joy'. There are times of struggle and darkness, times when we feel alone and lost but then the light of God breaks through and brings new life and hope. Desmond Tutu wrote these words in the period of Apartheid in South Africa:

> *Goodness is stronger than evil;*
> *Love is stronger than hate;*
> *Light is stronger than darkness;*
> *Life is stronger than death;*
> *Victory is ours through him who loves us.*

Love, peace & blessing, Chris.

21st MAY 2020

I have mixed feeling about this relaxing of Lockdown. The Government is sending out confused messages in the new rules (or lack of them).

We all understood what 'stay at home' meant, but what does 'Stay alert' mean? Will people maintain social distancing? How will people using public transport in our towns and cities respond? When will we be able to meet at church again? I am so missing congregational worship. I am told I can play golf but I can't go to church! It was recently pointed out to me that even when we can return in limited numbers, we won't be able to sing! I found this infinitely depressing. Methodists have always sung their theology. We have continued to do this at home by tuning into streamed services and *'Songs of Praise'* but it is not the same as being together in a sacred space and singing with those around you.

Today is Ascension Day. This morning I cycled to Christchurch. One of the independent coffee shops was selling takeaway drinks, so for the first time since Lockdown, I bought a 'proper' Americano and took it to Christchurch Priory grounds and sat on a bench in the shadow of this ancient building. It was very quiet and people-free. I became aware of a sense of peace enveloping me. I felt restored and I recalled the words of Psalm 23.

> *The Lord is my shepherd, I shall not want.*
> *He makes me lie down in green pastures;*
> *He leads me beside still waters;*
> *He restores my soul.*
> *He leads me in right paths for his names sake.*
> *Even though I walk through the darkest valley,*
> *I fear no evil; for you are with me.*

The Serenity Prayer written by Reinhold Niebuhr and published in 1951 is, I think, very apt for the present time.

> *God grant me the serenity to accept the things I cannot change, the courage to change the things I can and the wisdom to know the difference.*

Love, peace & blessing, Chris.

18th JUNE 2020

The news over this past week has been full of stories of violence: angry groups of antagonists, disruption of peaceful protests, disorder escalating. It seemed as if someone has put a match to people's pent-up feelings of frustration and disillusionment. Is Covid-19 exposing the hidden issues of injustice and deprivation?

I too have experienced anger, confusion, incredulity and anxiety over what has been happening. Our government has been trumpeting our 'world-beating' track and trace system. What arrogance! After spending millions, it is discovered not to work. We want no more slogans and false promises. A new normal cannot be built on lies and emptiness. I fear also that in the rush to get the economy going, things are moving too fast as non-essential businesses open up. In our Bournemouth area, pictures of the crowded beaches since last weekend suggest a lack of caution. I know people can't wait to get out and enjoy the good weather but the risks of infection seem to have been forgotten. Over 400 people died yesterday!

I am also angry over the way Boris keeps 'passing the buck'. He has now blamed Care Homes for the prevalence of Covid-19. Has the man any integrity? Why it is that powerful people attribute blame to others rather than to themselves? It happened in the Garden of Eden and has never ceased! (It wasn't me it was the woman! It wasn't me it was the snake!) Someone once said that there are four steps to wisdom: The ability to say:

1. I'm sorry
2. I don't know
3. I need help
4. I was wrong.

If those who govern are unable to say these things then I fear that our new normal will be much worse than our old.

Jesus, I get so angry at times that I do not know what to do with myself. I used to think that anger was a sin until I realised that you got angry too: angry at injustice, hypocrisy, and falsehood.

Redeem my anger so that it burns for righteousness: the wellbeing of the vulnerable

and the exposure of the corrupt.
May your grace and truth protect my soul
and make me whole. Amen

Love, peace & blessing, Chris.

23rd JUNE 2020

Christchurch Priory is at last open for private prayer. There is an excellent one-way system, with particular seats marked for visitor use. Tom and I were the only people there. Sitting quietly I again began to feel the silence and peace permeating my whole being. To be in this sacred space and soak up the Spirit of the prayer and liturgy which has drenched the walls of this ancient building was truly amazing. I was being fed. Although I have prayed at home for people in need, to be able to voice these prayers in this holy place and light a candle was so powerful. I wrote this prayer below to express some of the feelings I have had over the past weeks.

Lord God we come to you, how much our lives have changed.
How can we sing as once we did before?
Renew, restore us by your Spirit's power, enable us to feel you deep within.
We bring bewilderment, confusion too, hopes trashed, frustration rife.
Wonderings and doubts assail us now.
Protect us with your presence, love and peace.
We bring our fears, engendered by new rules; distorted views, paralysis within.
Help us to see that love must be our guide.
Give us compassion, wisdom, common sense.
We bring our sadness; so many have died; families unable to say goodbye. Struggles and suffering tearing them apart;

give them the strength and comfort that they need.
We bring our thanks; for time to stop and think;
for neighbours clapping; for zooming; hearing birds;
for sunshine, knowing you are with us Lord;
light in the darkness never overcome. Amen.

Love, peace & blessing, Chris.

26th JUNE 2020

Tom & I tune in to the Priory Morning Prayer on zoom most days. This week the Old Testament readings are from the book of Judges; a horrible book about violence, racism, genocide and war – not a comfortable read. In spite of God trying to save his peoples 'each person does what is right in their own eyes' with catastrophic results. Is that what is going to happen when lockdown finally ends? There is hope however beyond these reading from Judges. After this long nasty book comes the beautiful miniscule book of Ruth. There is no violence here. This is a story about inclusiveness, generosity, selfless love and the offer of hospitality to an outsider. It's about how one gracious act can plant seeds of hope for future generations.

After the darkness comes the light,
After exclusion comes embrace,
After tragedy comes the triumph,
After the famine comes the feast,
After death comes life.
Help me to travel in hope through the one,
in order to arrive at the other. Amen

Love, peace & blessing, Chris.

PART 3

A LESSON IN LOCKDOWN

Job learns about prayer

The book of Job[10] ponders the question, 'why does God allow disasters?' This righteous man has everything taken away from him, catches a terrible disease and goes into lockdown. He is depressed, angry and isolated - features we have already encountered in the letters of PART 2. Job is allowed visitors but these, instead of being a source of comfort, add to his distress. His situation, like ours during the pandemic, raises questions about the sort of God we believe in.

This study provides material for group discussion over a period of six weeks. To prepare for each meeting I suggest that, on your own, you read the appropriate chapters from the book of Job set out below.

1. Having a Hard Time   Chapters 1, 2, 3.
2. My Complaint   Chapters 21, 22, 23.
3. Where is Wisdom to be Found?   Chapters 27, 28, 31.
4. What Sort of God?   Chapters 32, 33, 38.
5. Behold my Creation   Chapters 39, 40, 41.
6. Understanding at Last   Chapter 42.

In your preparation, what do you make of the chapter you are reading? Make a note of this. When you gather together in your group, spend the first half hour sharing your personal comments before proceeding to the questions set.

1

HAVING A HARD TIME

*Then **Job** opened his mouth and said, ... 'Do not human beings have a hard service on earth...so I am allotted months of emptiness, and nights of misery are apportioned to me. When I lie down I say, "When shall I rise?" But the night is long, and I am full of tossing until dawn. My flesh is clothed with worms and dirt...Therefore I will not restrain my mouth; I will speak in the anguish of my spirit; I will complain in the bitterness of my soul...Will you not look away from me for a while, let me alone..! Why have you made me your target? Why have I become a burden to you?'*

Job 7 selected verses

*Then **Bildad** the Shuhite answered: 'How long will you say these things, and the words of your mouth be a great wind? Does God pervert justice?... If you will seek God and make supplication to the Almighty, if you are pure and upright, surely then he will rouse himself for you'.*

Job 8 selected verses.

The happy life Job once enjoyed was gone. His business empire had been devastated, his wealth lost and his children killed in a violent whirlwind; but that is not all. A loathsome disease attacks his body, eating into his flesh. He sits among the ashes and scrapes his sores with a piece of pottery.

The Prologue of the book (chapters 1 & 2) offers a theological explanation. His troubles are caused by Satan who argues that Job is not righteous because God has protected him from trouble. Take away that protection and 'he will curse you to your face' (1.11). God responds by allowing Satan to test him. 'Stretch out your hand against him', says the Lord (1.12 & 2.6). The Epilogue (chapter 42.7-17) brings Job's trial to a happy conclusion. While this nicely choreographed beginning and end may satisfy some, it is the middle 39 chapters of dialogue which pave the way for an exploration of the questions 'why does God allow disasters to happen to some people?' and 'what happens to people in lockdown?'

The date and origin of the book is unknown. It is also complicated by the fact that parts of the script have been added later. Furthermore, the text in some places is so hopelessly corrupt that translators have had to make educated guesses. Although the theological anguish of these central pages can reflect the Jewish experience of exile, Job was probably not a Jew and may not even have been in Babylon!

Three of his friends, Eliphaz, Bildad and Zophar (2.11) heard of his troubles and came to console him. When they saw him from a distance they did not recognise him and they raised their voices and wept. For seven days and nights they sat with him in silence 'for they saw that his suffering was very great' (2.13).

Covid-19 arrived here in the spring of 2020 derailing the normalities of life. Businesses folded. Visiting family members was prohibited. Hospital wards were filled to capacity. Every day the harsh reality of death touched the lives of thousands. The tardy reactions of Government did not allay confusion or remove the general sense of fear. Lockdown became an isolating experience for many. For those deprived of green spaces it proved to be even more disabling.

Although Job was able to have visitors, such was the horror of his condition that they could find no words of comfort. Finally Job speaks. Curses burst from his mouth (3.1). He vents bitter feelings of anguish. He wishes he had never been born. Strangulation and death is to be preferred (7.15). His prayer turns into a tirade of angry words directed at God whom he holds to be responsible for his terrible condition. 'Leave me alone! Stop tormenting me!'

Eliphaz, the first of Job's comforters, has tried to respond to Job's outrageous words by telling him that he should not be mouthing such terrible things (5.8). Job should humbly seek restoration from God who 'wounds, but binds up' (5.18). Job is now consumed by so much physical and emotional pain that he simply cannot hear this. Bildad next tries to restrain Job's unseemly avalanche of words which are 'a great wind' (8.2). He suggests that the root of Job's suffering must arise from some sin he has committed. If you sin, seek God and make supplication, God will 'restore to you your rightful place'. (8.4f).

To Ponder:
- How did you or someone you know cope with the isolation of lockdown and/or with the death of a close family member during lockdown?
- Was God responsible for the disasters Job had to endure? In what way might God be responsible for Covid-19?

2

MY COMPLAINT

*Then **Eliphaz** answered,... 'Is it for your piety that he reproves you, and enters into judgement with you? Is not your wickedness great? There is no end to your iniquities. For you have extracted pledges from your family for no reason, and stripped the naked of their clothing. You have given no water to the weary to drink, and you have withheld bread from the hungry....If you return to the Almighty, you will be restored, if you remove unrighteousness from your tents...'*

Job 22.4-7 & 23

*Then **Job** answered, 'Today also my complaint is bitter, his hand is heavy despite my groaning. O that I knew where I might find him that I might come even to his dwelling! I would lay my case before him, and fill my mouth with arguments...If I go forward, he is not there; or backwards, I cannot perceive him...But he knows the way that I take; when he has tested me, I shall come out like gold. My foot has held fast to his steps; I have kept his way and have not turned aside.*

Job 23.1-4, 8-11

Does God send disasters? I suggest that there are four ways of looking at the connection between God and the Covid pandemic.[11]

Secular   Covid-19 was an accidental event in Wuhan.

Determinist	God sent Covid -19.
Indirect	God allowed Covid-19.
Interpretive	Covid -19 is God's 'wake up' call.

The **secular** explanation leaves God right out of it. Disasters of this type arise because of the behaviour of human beings This is obvious when we think of how our rampageous destruction of the planet has given rise to climate change. Did the pandemic emerge because the normal processes of planetary life are being disrupted? Maybe! This does not necessarily exclude the possibility of something going wrong in a research establishment. Human suffering does follow from human wrongdoing, ignorance and the abandonment of justice.

Sin and suffering are related but not always in the causal ways we understand. I may not suffer directly because of my own extravagant lifestyle but those on the other side of the world may well experience the negative consequences of it. 3.7 million people, according to the World Health Organisation (2005), are dying each year from pollution. Toxic air levels in London and other urban areas are unhealthily high, yet we are still seduced by our 4x4 diesel vehicles.

A **determinist** explanation has validity if you read the Bible in a very literal way. There are countless examples of God sending or commanding people to do terrible things (Ex.12.29, Josh.8.1-2, Jud.16.28, 1Sam.15.2). This second option undermines human freedom and poses questions about the sort of God we believe in. God is just and holy but, as Jesus demonstrates, he is predominantly a God of grace and love. We have to dig behind the literal reading of these disturbing Old Testament texts.

The prologue of the book of Job hovers around the **indirect** explanation of 'God allowing'. God, in his act of creating, bestows the gift of freedom not only on human beings but on creation itself. In so doing God took a big risk in hoping that we would make the right choices. God cannot therefore escape ultimate responsibility for those negative consequences which occur when we mess things up. The supreme illustration of God's willingness to accept within Himself the human mess of failed human responsibility is displayed in the cross of Christ.

For the **interpretive** action explanation, you will have to wait until study 4 where I will suggest that this is the most appropriate response.

Over and against his three friends who insist that he must have done something wrong to merit such suffering, Job keeps reaffirming his innocence. Eliphaz now piles on the pressure and directly accuses Job of not pursuing justice. Has he ever stopped to think about where his wealth has come from? Surely he must have been involved in some form of exploitation of which he is unaware? Should he not have examined his affairs more closely? It is clear from chapter one that Job was righteous in all manner of religious observance (v.4-5) but we are not given any information at this stage about how he treated his neighbour. Has Eliphaz really put his finger on Job's sin? Not really, because Job later repudiates this charge (ch.31).

Job, however, has backed himself into a corner and will no longer listen to the arguments of his friends. As a last resort he decides to bring his case directly to Almighty God. He insists that he will be heard because of his suffering. But there is a new problem! God seems to have disappeared. In desperation he cries, 'O that I knew where I might find him!' (v.3). His praying has hit a brick wall.

While Job's comforters talk about righteousness Job **is** righteous because, unlike them, his troubles are so devastating that he is forced to let go of everything he is and was, including his faith in God. The cumulative effects of catastrophes piled on top of each other has obliterated the explanations which satisfy those of us who live securely and comfortably.

At the end of chapter 27 Job is exhausted, but so too is the debate. The theological road on which they have been travelling has ended in a blind alley. A radical change of perspective is required. This can only be discovered after an interval of waiting.

To Ponder:
- How do you explain the link between sin and suffering?
- May Eliphaz have been correct about Job not pursuing justice? Issues of social justice have largely fallen off the local church agenda. Why is this?
- What does losing your faith mean?

3

WHERE IS WISDOM TO BE FOUND?

*Surely there is a mine for silver, and a place for gold
to be refined. Iron is taken out of the earth, and copper
is smelted from ore. Miners put an end to darkness,
and search out to the farthest bound the ore in gloom
cvfdand deep darkness...They put their hand to the
flinty rock, and overturn mountains by their roots.
They cut out channels in the rocks, and their eyes see
every precious thing...But where shall wisdom be
found? And where is the place of understanding?
Mortals do not know the way to it, and it is not found
in the land of the living. The deep says, 'It is not in
me', and the sea says, 'It is not with me'. It cannot be
bought for gold, and silver cannot be weighed out as
its price...Abaddon and Death say, 'We have heard a
rumour of it with our ears.' God understands the way
to it, and he knows its place....When he made a decree
for the rain, and a way for the thunderbolt; then he
saw it and declared it; he established it and searched
it out. And he said to humankind, 'Truly, the fear of
the Lord, that is wisdom; and to depart from evil is
understanding.'*

Job 28 selected verses

This chapter is described in the NRSV as an 'interlude'. Is it
to be viewed as Job's own utterance or is it a later insertion into the
text in much the same way as the Prologue and Epilogue were
added?

The theme of the book of Job is not only about the impenetrable mystery of human suffering but about how we are to pray and speak of God in the midst of disaster. Job's friends, after an appropriate period of silence (2.13), do speak out. They are theologically trained to provide answers. Job rejects their explanations because their words serve only to add poignancy to the satanic attack. Orthodox theological answers have no validity when a person is abandoned, isolated, broken and wracked with pain. In such circumstances language collapses. Can wisdom be found in such an abyss?

Wisdom in the Hebraic tradition is not about intellectual cleverness but about acting with moral insight and integrity. The goal of wisdom is to create a harmonious and functional society reflecting the requirements of God. It is essentially practical and affects every department of life as is illustrated in the book of Proverbs. It is the Lord who gives wisdom; indeed wisdom has become a living personification of God in his act of creating (Proverbs 8). Wisdom is better than silver, gold and precious stones (8.10-11). That was why Solomon is such a significant figure in Wisdom Literature. How then do we find wisdom? Or rather, how do we allow wisdom to find us?

This chapter lists some of the places where people have looked. They have dug into the earth; cut channels in the rock; sought advice from birds and animals – but to no avail. In dark tunnels dug underground, miners have searched for gold and copper, but the treasure of wisdom has not been found. Job's dialogue with his three friends has shown him that wisdom is not found in orthodoxy either or in the tried and tested experience of the older generation. Neither is it discovered through human ingenuity or bought with gold (Proverbs 17.16). Wisdom is concealed from all living things; even from death itself. Should we conclude that we are no wiser after twenty three chapters of intensive debate? Not so! Something has happened because Job has acknowledged that God 'knows the way I take; when he has tried me, I shall come forth as gold' (23.10).

There is a further clue to the enigma of wisdom in this 'interlude'. Three quarters of chapter 28 tell of human beings searching and finding nothing; but from verse 23 a shift takes place. God's creating becomes the focus, 'He understands the way of it'. In the deep night of human search there is a hint of dawn.

We of the new creation know that wisdom has been revealed in Christ 'who is the power of God and the wisdom of God' (1 Cor.1.24). All darkness is dispelled in John's Gospel as the divine Word and Wisdom is revealed. The gift of wisdom is now available for all, according to James, who ask for it in faith (1.5f). This amazing truth was not realized in the experience of Job, but 'the way of it and the way to it' was glimpsed. Moreover the revelatory road was marked by two signposts: 'the fear of the Lord' and 'the need to depart from evil'.

To Ponder:

- What do you understand wisdom to be? Do you have it?
- In what ways can educational attainments add or detract from making you wise?

4

WHAT SORT OF GOD?

But when Elihu saw that there was no answer in the mouths of these three men, he became angry...'I am young in years and you are aged; therefore I was timid and afraid to declare my opinion to you....But now hear my speech, O Job, and listen to all my words...My words declare the uprightness of my heart, and what my lips know they speak sincerely. The spirit of God has made me, and the breath of the Almighty gives me life.

Job 32.5-6 & 33.1-4

Then the Lord answered Job out of the whirlwind: 'Who is this that darkens counsel by words without knowledge? Gird up your loins like a man, I will question you, and you shall declare to me. 'Where were you when I laid the foundations of the earth?

Job 38.1-3

Elihu suddenly bursts onto the stage in chapter 32. Eliphaz, Bildad and Zophar have nothing more to say in the face of Job's rebuttal. Elihu is young and full of words. He is angry because these old men have failed to convince Job of his error. Although he claims the divine inspiration of 'spirit' and 'breath', he more or less repeats what has already been said except for the end of his speech. His series of questions anticipate what is to come next. Why this additional insertion? The editor wishes to contrast the pretentious boisterous words of Elihu - with the whirlwind appearance of the LORD.

Some theologians,[12] like Job's comforters, have attempted to provide a rational explanation for 'why God allowed Covid-19'. The book of Job tends to dismiss this 'why?' question. Job has to learn that God does not provide answers; God poses questions and issues commands. The Bible is a book of action because God, the LORD, is not a noun to be discussed but a verb to propel – 'I will be what I will be' (Ex.3.14). Apart from the Prologue and Epilogue, this Yahweh word for God is used here for the first time,

Of the four possible explanations for Covid-19 in our study 2, the second and third may indeed be helpful to some, but they take us away from the question dynamic: 'what are we to do?' The required action, from the secular response, is to put in safeguards to prevent such a thing from happening again. God's revelation to Job encourages an **interpretive** action response.

God speaks to Job out of a whirlwind. Is it the same 'great wind' which struck down the house where his family were eating and drinking? God's terrifying epiphany explodes comfortable understandings of the sort of God we are dealing with. Because Christians call God 'Father' and see the friendly face of God in Jesus Christ, there is a tendency to dumb down the unpalatable aspects of the divine. The slogan 'God is love' can replace holiness with cosiness. Post-Enlightenment theology has a tendency to tame the terror and in so doing removes the wonder, stifles the imagination and paves the way for God to become a secular irrelevancy. All attempts to manage or explain the mystery of 'I AM' result in idolatry. The LORD will not be captured by our questions; instead

56

God demands action. The God revealed to Job has offered no closeness or intimacy but has driven him to a place of unknowing.

Elihu tells Job and his three friends to **listen** (33.1, 34.1). The LORD, on the other hand, tells Job to **look**. But where is Job to look? He must first look into the darkness and 'take it to its territory' and 'find its home' (38.19-21). Job has several times spoken of darkness. There is darkness on the day of his birth (3.3-4). On his death he will return to the land of gloom and deep darkness (10.21-22). He complains that God has broken him and set darkness upon his path (19.8). He is terrified of meeting God and desires only to 'vanish in darkness' (23.15f). When Yahweh finally appears he accuses Job of 'darkening' counsel with words without knowledge (38.2).

It is through the contemplation of blinding darkness that light comes. It is an Exodus equivalent of Calvary. Redemption comes from a night of deep darkness beyond explanation and thought in a place of unknowing. The Christian mystic of the sixteenth century, St John of the Cross, tells us that 'the dark night is God's best gift to us, intended for our liberation'.

To Ponder:
- Have you ever been in a spiritually dark place where God seems absent? What did you do?
- Christians tend to focus on the resurrection rather than on the cross; on light rather than darkness. Is this why our spirituality is not as deep or as enabling as it could be?

5

BEHOLD MY CREATION

'Have you commanded the morning since your days began, and caused the dawn to know its place? ... Have you comprehended the expanse of the earth? Declare, if you know this. Where is the way to the dwelling of light, and where is the place of darkness?...Can you bind the chains of the Pleiades, or loose the cords of Orion?... Do you know the ordinances of the heavens? Can you establish their rule on the earth?'

Job 38 selected verses

'Do you know when the mountain goats give birth?...Who has let the wild ass go free?... Is the wild ox willing to serve you? Will it spend the night at your crib?... Do you give the horse it's might?...Do you make it leap like the locust?...Is it at your command that the eagle mounts up and makes its nest on high?'

Job 39 selected verses

And the LORD said to Job... 'Anyone who argues with God must respond'. Then Job answered the LORD: 'See I am of small account; what shall I answer you?'... Then the Lord answered Job out of the whirlwind: 'Gird up your loins like a man; I will question you, and you declare to me'.

Job 40.1-7

PART 3 A Lesson in Lockdown

Look at Behemoth, which I made just like you; it eats grass like an ox... It makes its tail stiff like a cedar; the sinews of its thighs are knit together...Can you draw out Leviathan with a fish-hook, or press down its tongue with a cord?...Who can open the doors of its face? There is terror all around its teeth.

Job 40.15f & 41 selected verses

Eliphaz, Bildad, Zophar and Elihu offer Job explanations. Yahweh does not! Instead of theological answers God bombards Job with a list of questions – over forty of them. The first group are cosmological as God tests out Job's knowledge of the heavens, the stars and the earth (38.4-38). In the second set God examines him on what he knows about lions, goats, donkeys, oxen, the ostrich, the horse, the hawk, the hippopotamus and the crocodile (38.39 - 40.24). Linked with these questions is the implicit instruction to observe, look and investigate. This avalanche of relentless interrogation sweeps away Job's agenda. Indeed halfway through the zoological examination God wants Job to say something but he cannot find the words. 'I lay my hand on my mouth' (40.3). The LORD, who is clearly exasperated by Job's refusal to argue, shouts out of the whirlwind, 'Gird up your loins like a man; I will question you'. Job can hide no longer. He must reply.

The ordering of God's questions to Job from chapter 38 takes us back to the opening chapters of Genesis: the darkness and light (v.9 & 12), the sea and the firmament (v.8-1), the earth and the stars (v.26 & 31) and finally the animals (v.39f). These references to the heavens and the creatures of earth also take us directly to Psalm 8 where humankind is given responsibility **for** 'the sheep, oxen, the beasts of the field, the birds of the air and whatever passes along the paths of the sea'. According to one Rabbi, when God had finished creating he showed Adam all the glories of nature and said, 'Behold the beauty of this world. I am handing it over to you. Be careful that you do not damage it, for if you do, there will be no one left to mend it.'[13]

While Job's comforters may have been theologically correct in spelling out timeless truths, they are wrong because they ignore the real-life context. Creation and planetary life is that context.

Has Job become another Adam tempted by Satan? Adam disobeyed and driven from the garden lost the blessing; Job, tested to the point of destruction, regained the blessing. The LORD's relentless cross-examination of Adam's successor centres on two fundamental questions: 'Who are you?' and 'Where were you?'(Gen.3.9). Job's response to the identity question is, 'I am of small account' (40.3). But is he? The Psalmist confronts this pessimistic picture by telling us that, although humans are 'a little lower than the divine beings', we are above creation. We are **not** of small account!'

Job has lost this realization and moans, 'what are human beings that you make so much of them, that you set your mind on them?' (7.17-21). God now confronts this grovelling attitude and give us the key message of the Old Testament namely, that **whether or not we have faith in God, God has faith in us.**[14]

Job is discovering that God never explains and seldom gives answers but rather commands us to observe, question, learn and then do what it necessary. It is through our obedience that we not only discover some of the answers but may indeed find our true identity.

To Ponder:

- If God said to you 'who are you and where are you?' What would you say?
- God seldom gives answers but rather questions and commands. Do you agree?
- Have you grasped this supreme truth that it is not our faith in God which is of supreme important but rather it is God's faith in us?

6

UNDERSTANDING AT LAST

Then Job answered the LORD: 'I know that you can do all things, and that no purpose of yours can be thwarted. "Who is this that hides counsel without knowledge?" Therefore I have uttered what I did not understand, things too wonderful for me, which I did not know. "Hear, and I will speak; I will question you, and you declare to me." I had heard of you by the hearing of the ear, but now my eye sees you; therefore I despise myself, and repent in dust and ashes.'

Job 42.1-6

The LORD said to Eliphaz the Temanite: 'My wrath is kindled against you and against your two friends; for you have not spoken of me what is right, as my servant Job has'...And the LORD restored the fortunes of Job when he had prayed for his friends; and the LORD gave Job twice as much as he had before...In all the land there were no women so beautiful as Job's daughters...

Job 42.7,10-11,15

Job has wanted to argue his case with the Almighty. When God finally gave him an opportunity, he does not know what to say (40.1-5). In chapter 42 he eventually speaks. His words take the form of a confession. The LORD has accused him of darkening counsel by words 'without knowledge' (38.2). Job takes this very phrase and plays it back. When Yahweh reveals himself, human language is transcended. The insertion of the Yahweh sentence 'I will question you, and you declare to me', previously addressed to a tongue-tied Job in 40.7 is a further illustration of how divine speech must be truly absorbed and totally inhabit human language if revelation is to be apprehended. When this happens, language creates a new 'seeing'.

Today's important theological task is to find words with which to speak of God to the rich and powerful from global contexts of war, starvation, the displacement of millions of people, climate change, refugees and governments who put the interests of themselves and their cronies before the common good.[15]

Job confesses 'I despise (loathe) myself'. This translation is not necessarily correct since the word 'myself' is not in the Hebrew text. It is suggested that the interpretation could be 'I loathe *my words'*. This affects the final sentence about 'in dust and ashes'. The word 'ashes' is present in the book's opening demonstration of mourning (2.8, 12). The only other Biblical reference to 'dust and ashes' is in the story of Abraham beseeching God to save the city of Sodom (Gen 18.27). Job is not engaging here in an act of self-abasement by repenting 'in' dust and ashes but rather, like Abraham – the man of faith, Job has become fully aware of **'being'** dust and ashes.[16]

The usual interpretation of this confession is that God's dramatic appearance is so awesome and majestic that Job is squashed. In fact the **opposite** is true. Job is rather repenting of a grovelling 'dust and ashes' mentality. As the previous dialogues proceeded up to chapter 31 he kept repudiating his status as a victim. With God's appearance, however, he slips back into a subservient attitude so that the LORD has to command him to 'Gird up your loins like a man' (40.6). There must be no 'woe is me' attitude. God is commanding him to be bold, to stand tall, to refuse to take 'no' for an answer and to affirm, as St Paul did in the New Testament: 'I can do all things through him who strengthens me' (Phil.4.13).

This is Job's righteousness. He stands before God not as a victim but as a victor. His friends, mouthing traditional orthodox theology, may have satisfying answers to the 'why' question but they are wrong because they do not confront God! We are not to be dust and ashes in God's presence; we must demand a hearing. Job is a new Abraham whose relentless bargaining prayers over Sodom made God 'change his mind'. This is why Job, in the Epilogue, can intercede for his friends and save them from being punished for their folly (v.8-9). The LORD's rebuke of Eliphas in chapter 22 verses 26-30 is a wonderful piece of irony. He had told Job that if he sought to be reconciled to God, he would become an 'intercessor who would deliver the guilty from divine wrath' Job did the opposite. He refused to submit and instead choose to challenge the very nature of God's providence and by so doing he **becomes** an intercessor.

The message of the book of Job is that we are made in the image of God and set within his creation as stewards to observe, understand, care and act responsibly. This is our vocation. It is an outworking of God's faith in us. In the presence of injustice, catastrophe and destruction it is never right to be passive or to remain silent. As divine intercessors we are to argue with God and with anyone who adopts a victim mentality or fatefully accepts that disaster, injustice and ruin are 'the normal'.

The book of Job teaches us that in situations of lockdown, pandemic, war or climate catastrophe God demands that we stand up, argue, act and challenge the empty words of those who attempt to silence us. Above all our prayers must hold God to account!

To Ponder:

- When did you last have an argument with God? Who won?
- When should we say 'Thy will be done'?
- Has lockdown made you more aware of other people and of the problems of the wider world? If not, why not? If so, what are you doing about it?

WHAT HAVE YOU LEARNT ABUT YOUR LOCKDOWN
FROM THIS STUDY OF JOB?

PART 4

Letters of Liberation

Normal life for Job had been destroyed. His friends seek to comfort him in lockdown by providing reasons for his tragic condition. Finally, God appears; but still no answers. Nevertheless this is the turning point and Job emerges from lockdown. Unfortunately there is no information on how he made it to the new normal. We only know he got there.

These letters may fill some of the gaps. Christine's Lockdown Letters record emotions of fear, frustration and anger at the behaviour of others, not excluding the Government, who like Job's comforters, got many things wrong. On the positive side her letters affirm the renewing power of nature. Job was told to contemplate the wonders of creation. Christine leaves us in no doubt that our natural world is a source of revelation and renewal.

These letters take us forward, even though the journey to full liberation is disrupted by the second lockdown. Here we exchange fear for faith and discover the joy of again being part of the wider community.

24th JULY 2020

I was thinking back to December when we first heard of the Wuhan virus. Little did we anticipate the effect it would have on all our lives. I remember telling myself that it wouldn't really affect us. I assumed it would go away! How wrong I was. Over the past months my way of life has changed.

I have had to learn patience and tolerance. I have had to learn how to re-plan my days and give them purpose. I have found myself thinking more about our neighbours and other local people who are really struggling. How can I support them? I have had to learn to sit and be, rather than rush about from thing to thing. I have had to confront my fears about going out, respecting social distancing and trusting others. I have become more thankful for the many things I used to take for granted.

On Sunday we attended Christchurch Priory which has at last opened up for Sunday worship. I went with some trepidation, wondering what it would be like. It was such a positive experience! It was good to recognise the familiar faces – even with masks on – of those we had seen on Zoom. It was wonderful to hear the magnificent organ even though we could not sing. It was breathtaking to experience the liturgy and participate in the Communion. We could only receive the bread, so when Charles - the vicar - blessed and drank the wine we responded with a loud AMEN. I felt very included.

To compensate for our inability to sing in church, Tom and I sing our hearts out at home when we replay *Songs of Praise* later in the day! In Ephesians 3, St. Paul writes of 'the boundless riches of Christ' and prays.

> *I ask that you may be strengthened in your inner being with power through his Spirit, and that Christ may dwell in your hearts through faith, as you are being rooted and grounded in love. I pray that you may have the power to understand what is the breadth, length, height and depth*

*and to know the love of Christ so that you may be filled
with all the fullness of God.*

**These wonderful words of hope and assurance make me
realise that God is more with us than we are with him.**

Love, peace & blessing, Chris.

14th AUGUST 2020

Tom and I drove to Yeovil in Somerset to visit my brother,
sister-in-law and niece. It was the longest drive we have had
since early March! It felt like an adventure. We have become
so insular over the past months. Even doing the simple things
we have not done for some time takes courage. Lockdown has
left a legacy of fear.

Some of my friends are finding leaving the house a real
challenge. I recently spoke to a lady who said she has not
been in a shop since March and was still too scared to go out.
I suppose it is easier to stay cocooned at home, but what
about faith?

We must not think of ourselves as victims of the pandemic.
We are called to be victors like Job.

Yesterday's terrific thunderstorm with torrential rain flooded
the road outside our house and made a lake of our garden. It
reminded me of last Sunday's Gospel reading; the story of
Peter walking on the waves. Attempting to be with Jesus
meant leaving the safe place and stepping out into the storm.
Peter began well but instead of keeping his eyes on Jesus
looked at the waves. Gripped by fear he starts to sink. But
Jesus was there to save him.

I am part of a Sunflower Challenge with two of my friends –
Liz and her brother, John. At the moment, mine is 7 feet high
and beginning to flower. I am quite proud of it. It would have

68

been better if I had fed it instead of just leaving it to get on as best it could. Liz told me her sunflower is nearly 8 feet. She must have fed it and given it more care. Will the squirrel eat off the head of mine as it did a few years ago? The fascinating thing about sunflowers is that they turn their faces during the day to follow the direction of the sun. We should be doing the same and turn our faces to follow the SON!

> *Dear Jesus, help me to fix my gaze on you.*
> *I admire Peter because he stepped out with courage*
> *and faith.*
> *Help me to do the same and also to know*
> *that you will always be with me. Amen*

Love, peace & blessing, Chris.

21st AUGUST 2020

Tom and I have had some very special days this week. On Sunday evening our family from Manchester (Matthew, Jane and their children Oliver and Lucy) arrived. We have not seen them for nearly a year. Our first hugs! So emotional! They had booked into the local Premier Inn as our bungalow is small and they did not want to inconvenience us.

Jane, our daughter-in-law, had arranged belated surprise celebrations for Tom's 80th birthday. She had hired a hut for Monday on the Avon Beach. When she told me of this a week ago I was anxious. The weather forecast for Monday was heavy rain and thunderstorms! Thankfully the storms did not materialise. From the moment they arrived till when they left on Tuesday the sun shone brightly. It was a miracle occasion. Sitting on the beach our son Matt said, 'This is the first time I have been able to forget Covid-19.' (He's a caretaker in a school which had remained open for Keyworkers' children). It was also a wonderful day because our grandson Oliver overcame his fears and went into the sea for the first time.

Lounging in deck chairs, with no one nearby, we enjoyed the afternoon swimming and building sandcastles. Jane, who had been furloughed, continually supplied us with food and drinks served on the bone china which she had brought with her all the way from Manchester! She had also decorated the hut in honour of the octogerian. The day ended with fish and chips of course! An occasion of refreshment, freedom and fun!

I hope there will be days like that for you now that even more restrictions are being lifted. What a joy it is to be physically present with those we love and who demonstrate such imaginative care and understanding.

Thank you, Jesus, for blessing us through our family. Amen

Love, peace & blessing, Chris.

18th SEPTEMBER 2020

On Sunday Tom preached at the Priory about Joseph: *The Bigger Picture.* It was a good message reminding us not to be afraid but to live in hope.

Our daughter, Jo, came by train from Ilford via Waterloo on Monday to stay overnight. It's the first time we had seen her since March. What a delight to have her here, to catch up with her news and to exchange hugs. Although we have talked and seen each other most days on *WhatsApp* this was something very special.

The schools have opened. Our granddaughter, Lucy (8), was so pleased to be with her friends again. Jane, (our daughter-in-law) is also back at work. Our grandson, Oliver, has started Secondary School. He is very anxious. There must be lots of other children and parents who are fearful. O dear! After two days he has been sent home with the rest of his Year Group because one of the pupils had tested positive. Change in his routine is something he cannot cope with.

This morning Tom and I walked round Hengistbury Head. We looked over Poole Bay and saw four gigantic cruise liners moored. What does the future hold for them and for the tourist industries?

At one point on our walk we stopped enthralled by a murmuration of starlings as they rose to perform their aerial acrobatics. It's as if they are held by an invisible thread which binds them together with one mind! I couldn't help thinking how as Christians, we too are held together by the invisible thread of the Holy Spirit who leads, gathers us together in harmony and makes us soar with exuberant love. As Tom said on Sunday 'There is a better story and a bigger picture'.

Love, peace & blessing, Chris.

23rd OCTOBER 2020

Did you see Maureen from Barnsley on the television? When asked for her reaction to South Yorkshire entering the Tier 3 of lockdown, this 83-year-old great-grandmother said exactly what was in her heart; no waffle, no political correctness, no avoiding the issue. She was someone who had grasped life with both hands and wanted to live without being paralyzed by fear. Her main concern was for the next generation. 'I'll be dead soon but they will be left with the fallout and have to pay for it'. It was so refreshing to hear her rather than the bland comments of Government ministers.

Love, peace & blessing, Chris.

6th November 2020

HERE WE ARE IN OUR SECOND LOCKDOWN – not so well defined as the first but with our lives again restricted. I am particularly upset by the closure of churches after all the hard work done to keep people safe. Last Wednesday, just before this Lockdown, I met a friend for coffee in a nearby garden centre. There were so many people – most of them without masks – buying Christmas fripperies, creating long queues and forgetting all about social distancing. The decision to shut places of worship – where the rules were being kept – simply reflects our secular society where materialism and consumerism takes priority over spiritual wellbeing.

This morning Tom and I cycled into Christchurch to go to the Priory, which is still open for private prayer. We were the only visitors. As we left we both commented on the sublime stillness. The very prayers of the worshipers over the centuries had somehow soaked into these ancient walls. Where is your special place of renewal and release?

Love, peace & blessing, Chris.

20th NOVEMBER 2020

Yesterday, Tom and I walked in the woods at Rhinefield near Brockenhurst. It was a crisp clear morning. The light from the weak sun seemed to be painting the trees with magic. We walked in the shadow of the towering redwoods. I hugged one of the majestic sequoias. It would take more the 10 people holding hands to span their enormous girth. We must keep physically connecting ourselves with the healing spirit which permeates the natural world of trees, rocks and plants. These wonderful redwoods and sequoias evoke awe and wonder. They give us a realistic perspective. They will be here when Tom and I are long gone.

Today we learn of yet another government minister who has breached parliamentary rules but has neither resigned nor been taken to task. I get exasperated and upset. One rule for them and another for us. Do our leaders have no integrity? I also do not understand why we have to have 'state of the art weapons' when hundreds are dying each day from the pandemic; when increasing numbers of families are living in poverty and when more and more people are losing their jobs and livelihoods. Although I did gain a renewed perspective at Rhinefield amongst the trees, it still doesn't solve the problems around us.

Yesterday afternoon following a storm, there was the most amazing rainbow. I haven't seen such a complete bow for ages. I recognised it as a promise of hope! I looked up Genesis 9 in my Bible where God says, 'I have set my bow in the clouds and it shall be a sign of the covenant between me and all the earth'. I immediately thought of that old hymn 'O love that wilt not let me go'.

> *O joy that seekest me through pain,*
> *I cannot close my heart to thee:*
> *I trace the rainbow through the rain,*
> *and feel the promise is not vain,*
> *that morn shall tearless be'.*

Love, peace & blessing, Chris.

11ᵗʰ DECEMBER 2020

When I turned on the news this morning, the first report was not about the pandemic or Brexit but about Barbara Windsor's death. She had suffered from Alzheimer's disease for six years which was so sad when I recall the 'Carry-On' films. She brought such a sense of naughty fun to the screen. Laughter is a healer. It drags us from the doldrums and lifts us to a happy place. It's contagious. If you see others spontaneously laughing wholeheartedly it's almost impossible not to smile. There hasn't been much to laugh about over these last months. A good dose of it keeps us sane!

Our Manchester family are Roman Catholics and on Thursday evening our granddaughter Lucy received her First Communion. This should have happened in June when we had planned to be present as we were for her brother Oliver a few years ago. We have received photos. Lucy looks amazing in her white dress. It was such a special occasion for her. We pray that this experience will have lasting effects and grow into a living faith.

We will soon to be lighting the third Advent candle. As we journey towards Christmas, the lighting of an additional candle each week increases hope until it culminates in the lighting of all five candles on Christmas night. Tom and I will be on our own this Christmas. It will still be a very special time of joy because light is coming into the world and we shall be together to experience that light!

Light illuminating our anxious times with hope.
Light transmitting energy to love, to struggle for justice,
to share what we have, to smile, to laugh
and anticipate a new tomorrow. Amen

Love, peace & blessing, Chris.

8th JANUARY 2021

I hope you are all keeping safe now we are once again back in lockdown. What a strange year we have had! There is still much uncertainty about the future. When will we be able to meet together and give each other a hug? Will the vaccination programme be achieved by the summer? Will our churches be open and the sound of congregational singing be heard again? Will our masks be discarded and thrown away? Will our young people return to school and college knowing their education will not be interrupted?

I was feeling a bit overwhelmed with questions and doubts when Tom, quite out of the blue, said, 'Let's go to Hengistbury Head'. This is something the new rules allow. For me it's a very special place. It was blowing a gale. The sea was wild. The sun was shining brilliantly. As I walked round the top, I felt God once again sweeping away my confused thoughts and inner unrest. This is a place of healing. Whenever I go there my spiritual wellbeing is renewed. We all need to find our special place – what Celtic Christians call 'a thin place' – where the spirit world breaks through into our earthly physical existence.

This reminded me that on Wednesday we shall be celebrating the Feast of the Epiphany, which focuses on the Wise Men who journeyed to the manger. I immediately thought of something I had read long ago.

If the 3 Wise Men had been 3 Wise Women they'd have:
asked directions,
got there on time,
taken the right presents,
cleaned the stable,
made a casserole
and left peace on earth!

Love, peace & blessing, Chris.

22ⁿᵈ JANUARY 2021

This morning on my daily walk I came across a hazelnut tree displaying the most wonderful show of yellow catkins. Some of the snowdrops in our garden are opening a little more each day. I get so excited when these pure white flowers appear once again. The sight gives me the assurance of Spring even in the midst of the uncertainty and anxiety around us.

What a week it has been; the number of infections, the huge figures of deaths reported. It is staggering and horrifying, but on the positive side the vaccines are being rolled out. I hope there will be a large uptake evenly distributed and that the administering of the vaccine will prove to be efficient and effective.

Wasn't it refreshing to see the new President of the US inaugurated! I felt so relieved that there were no hitches. His speech was very uplifting, offering hope and healing for the people of America.

Tom will be preaching again at the Priory. It will be Candlemas. As a Methodist, I had never heard of it. When Tom told me it related to Simeon and Anna's experience of personal illumination in the temple I thought, 'That's good news for us all.'

Love, peace & blessing, Chris.

19th MARCH 2021

Yesterday I walked around Christchurch Quay. Lots of people were doing the same. On the Priory Lawns a group of pre-school children were having a wonderful time playing with hoops; great fun when you are under-five. I still find real pleasure in doing simple things.

Spring is most definitely with us. Aren't the daffodils amazing this year? They are everywhere: by the side of the roads, on roundabouts, clusters near hedgerows. They raise our spirits by their sheer exuberance. They make me want to dance and sing.

We are approaching Passion Sunday, when Jesus begins the long and final journey to the cross. Why Passion? Passion is the expression of a deep feeling, something we have seen recently with the responses to the murder of Sarah Everard. Passion is full of deep emotion and pain. Jesus reveals this when he weeps at the tomb of Lazarus his friend, cries over Jerusalem, prays in Gethsemane and dies on the cross. This passion of extravagant love can touch the hearts of all of us.

What are you passionate about? I am passionate about music. I haven't always felt this, but I do now. I had never enjoyed the music of J.S. Bach but in 1990, Tom took me to a performance of Bach's St. Matthew Passion at the Royal Albert Hall. In his student days he used to go, every year on Passion Sunday, to the Festival Hall and hear it in English performed big-time by the Bach Choir conducted by Reginald Jacques.

Fifty years later, when we took our seat he was so disappointed. He hadn't realised that the performance style had changed so radically. This time it was in German with tiny orchestras and small choirs. They were using a chamber organ rather than the gigantic Albert Hall organ. He sadly sat beside me trying to smile. I think he felt he had let me down.

I was spellbound! The music conveyed such joy and hope. It entered my soul. I saw. I heard. I felt and I knew. The wonderful world of J.S. Bach suddenly opened up. I have never looked back.

> *See Him! Whom? The Bridegroom Christ.*
> *See Him! How? The spotless Lamb.*
> *Come ye daughters share my mourning.*
>
> *While life shall last, O Let Thy sufferings claim our love,*
> *Since Thou for us salvation sure hast wrought.*

Love, peace & blessing, Chris.

16th APRIL 2021

I felt really sad about the death of Prince Philip. He has been there all my life and given the country so much. His 'off the cuff' comments and political incorrectness banished the stuffiness of royalty and state. The Queen and Prince Philip, in their long life together, have preserved their integrity and demonstrated a persistent sense of duty. They have also had their share of family problems, all in the public eye, yet have maintained their dignity. I was amused and impressed that Prince Philip designed his own funeral carriage on a Land Rover!

On Sunday Tom and I went to the Priory. Towards the end of the service we were all invited to go outside and stand (socially distanced and unmasked) on the spacious Priory Lawns, to sing the closing hymn:

> *Love's redeeming work is done,*
> *Fought the fight, the battle won;*
> *Vain the stone, the watch, the seal'*
> *Christ has burst the gates of hell;*
> *Alleluia!*

CHRIST IS RISEN! HE IS RISEN INDEED!

Love, peace & blessing, Chris.

14th MAY 2021

I have made the decision to discontinue these weekly epistles. I started writing to you on a weekly basis at the beginning of April 2020. It's been a privilege and a joy keeping this contact. I've been able to share my thoughts and have appreciated your responses. We have encouraged each other to cope with the lockdowns. Tiers, frustrations and anger; these have come and gone! From Monday next we can enjoy the new relaxation of restrictions. Hopefully all will go as planned. I am really looking forward to physically meeting up with you all before long.

Last Sunday Tom preached at the Priory about *Pruning and Growing*. He concluded by reflecting on lockdown and said, 'A pruning and emptying process has taken place. A Holy Spirit filling is now required.'

Yesterday was Ascension Day, when the disciples were told by Jesus to wait for the Holy Spirit's outpouring. As Jesus was taken into heaven they must have been looking up in wonder. They were beholding something of the glory of God. The Ascension was a rounding off of Jesus' earthly ministry. He is leaving them to get on with the work of waiting and witness so that the Kingdom of God could be born in the hearts, minds and communities of people everywhere. He did not leave us unequipped. The promised Holy Spirit came. If we are open and ready, that same Spirit will come to us to take us on to a new normal and a fresh chapter in our lives.

> *Come down, O Love divine,*
> *Seek thou this soul of mine,*
> *And visit it with thine own ardour glowing;*
> *O Comforter, draw near,*
> *Within my heart appear,*
> *And kindle it, thy holy flame bestowing.*

Love, peace & blessing, Chris.

PART 5

IN AND OUT OF LOCKDOWN

Jonah - a man who learns nothing

Christine's letters have taken us in and out of lockdown. The book of Jonah[17] does the same, as did my short sermon on Elijah.

These four studies provide material for group discussion. Chapter 1 describes how, in attempting to escape God's commission, Jonah is plunged into lockdown. His lockdown experience, described in chapter 2, is unique; he spends three days and nights tangled up in sea-weed buried in the belly of a 'big fish'. Time to reflect!

In chapter 3 Jonah is released from his fishy lockdown and now decides to do as he was commanded. Chapter 4 parallels chapter 2 in being another reflective episode except that this time his lockdown is self imposed. He cannot return to the old normal; neither does he know how to move forward into a new normal.

My original study on Jonah was first published by the Methodist Church in 2018 for their annual Bible Month. This resulted in a number of day conferences. Just before lockdown I began, though could not finish, the four sessions in Christchurch Priory.

The study has been totally re-written for this publication.

1

GETTING INTO LOCKDOWN

(1) Now the word of the LORD came to Jonah the son of Amittai, saying, (2) 'Go at once to Nineveh, that <u>great</u> city, and cry against it; for their wickedness has come up before me.' (3) But Jonah set out to flee to Tarshish from the presence of the LORD. He went down to Joppa and found a ship going to Tarshish; so he paid his fare and went on board (goes down), to go with them to Tarshish, away from the presence of the LORD.

(4) But the LORD hurled a <u>great</u> wind upon the sea, and such a mighty storm came upon the sea that the ship threatened to break up. (5) Then the mariners were afraid, and each cried to his god. They threw the cargo that was in the ship into the sea, to lighten it for them. Jonah, meanwhile, had gone down into the hold of the ship and had lain down, and was fast asleep. (6) The captain came and said to him, 'What are you doing sound asleep? Get up, call on your god! Perhaps the god will spare us a thought so that we do not perish.'

(7) The sailors said to one another, 'Come, let us cast lots, so that we may know on whose account this calamity has come upon us.' So they cast lots, and the lot fell upon Jonah. (8) Then they said to him, 'Tell us, why this calamity has come upon us? What is your occupation? And where do you come from? What is your

country? And of what people are you?' (9) 'I am a Hebrew.' He replied. 'I worship the LORD, the God of heaven, who made the sea and the dry land.' (10) Then the men <u>feared with a great fear</u>, and said to him, 'What is this that you have done!' For the men knew that he was fleeing from the presence of the LORD, because he had told them so.

(11) Then they said to him, 'What shall we do to you, that the sea may quieten down for us?' For the sea was growing more and more tempestuous. (12) He said to them, 'Pick me up and throw me into the sea; then the sea will quieten down for you; for I know it is because of me that this <u>great</u> storm has come upon you.' (13) Nevertheless, the men rowed hard to bring the ship back to land, but they could not, for the sea grew more and more stormy against them. (14) Then they cried out to the LORD, 'Please, O LORD, we pray, do not let us perish on account of this man's life. Do not make us guilty of innocent blood; for you, O LORD, have done as it pleased you.' (15) So they picked Jonah up and threw him into the sea; and the sea ceased from its raging.

(16) Then the men feared the LORD <u>with a great fear</u> and they offered a sacrifice to the LORD and made vows.

The book of Jonah begins, like some of the smaller Old Testament prophetic books (Hosea 1.1, Joel 1.1, Micah 1.1, Zephaniah 1.1) with an announcement; 'The word of the Lord came to Jonah'. Instead of mentioning oracles or visions (Isaiah 1.1, Nahum 1.1, Malachi 1.1) the very first word of the Hebrew text is *way^{e}hi,* literally translated, 'And it happened'. This sends a signal to the Jewish reader, and also to us, that we are dealing with story rather than with factual history. Although a prophet called Jonah did exist (2 Kings 14.25-28) he is a hazy figure, a bit like Robin Hood and King Arthur. This story is the stuff of legend.

The writer/storyteller, in relating this naughty parody of a prophet, knows how to hold his audience spellbound through his use of genre, image, drama, suspense and irony. It is there from the very beginning. Instead of travelling northeast to Nineveh as commanded, Jonah goes southwest on an ocean cruise heading for Tarshish – a maritime area somewhere in the direction of Spain.

Why does Jonah disobey and flee from the LORD? The narrator doesn't tell us. We have to work it out for ourselves. He also teases us. 'The men knew that he was fleeing from the presence of the LORD, because he had told them so' (v.10). Jonah has told the sailors but he has not told us. He is deliberately keeping us in suspense. Like a good detective novel it is only in the last chapter that the shocking truth is revealed.

One of the most recurring words used (which I have underlined in the text) is 'great' or 'big' (1.2, 1.4, 1.12, 16, 17; 3.1, 3.5; 4.11). The frequency of 'big' is compounded by the fact that in Hebrew there are no adverbs so that the literal translation of 'they feared exceedingly' (1.10, 16) is 'they feared with a great fear'. See how this same Hebraism is present in Mark 4.41.

Joppa was the location of his of embarkation. This is the same Mediterranean port where, in the New Testament, the apostle Peter received his vision of God's all-embracing mission (Acts 10). He, like Jonah, was not keen on doing what God wanted.

Jonah not only disobeyed God by going west instead of east, he goes 'down' rather than 'up'. He first 'goes down' to Joppa, then 'down' to the ship. When the storm breaks he goes 'down' into the belly of the ship and lay 'down' to sleep. He was to discover that there was no getting away from this God of earth and sea who pursues him relentlessly. Jonah is starting to pay the price (note *fare*) for his disobedience. Not allowing Jonah to escape, God 'hurled' a great wind upon the sea. The word 'hurl' conjures up a violent image. The narrator uses this word several times. The sailors 'hurl' the cargo overboard before they finally 'hurl' the prophet into the abyss. We have already, in our study of Job, met this terrifying God who sweeps people away in a whirlwind.

Unlike Job who argues with God, Jonah says nothing! He refuses to vent his frustration. In a state of total denial he hides and even sleeps while this horrendous hurricane threatens to destroy everything and everyone. His refusal to face reality or even to pray prompts the desperate captain to search him out, wake him up and shout, 'What are you doing sleeping at a time like this?' Sailors are very superstitious. Someone on board must have caused the storm. Jonah is identified through the casting of lots. In a morbid conference he is subjected to intense interrogation. Why? What? Where? Who? Finally all the questions culminate in the key question 'What shall we do with you?' Jonah has hitherto maintained his silence but now the whole sorry story spills out. This only serves to increase the anxiety of the sailors.

The word Jonah uses for God is the holy name LORD (*Yahweh*) - first revealed to Moses (Ex.3.14). The sailors worship a plethora of different deities translated here by the Hebrew word *Elohim* (literally 'gods'). Both words occur many times in this book. What is impressive about this religious interchange is the openness of the sailors over and against the buttoned-up attitude of Jonah. In the ministry of Jesus we also discover that 'outsiders' are often more open to compassion and truth than 'the religious insiders' (Lk.8.5-13, 19.1-10). Jesus speaks of the 'sign of Jonah' (Matt.12.38-42, 16.1-4, Lk.11.29-32) to pass judgment upon the closed minds of the Pharisees and the Sadducees. They were his contemporary 'Jonahs'.

Although Jonah has brought disaster upon them all, the sailors still want to save him. They again take to the oars in a final frantic attempt to bring the ship to land. Their efforts prove futile. God simply ratchets up the storm. Finally and reluctantly they give in to Jonah's request and 'hurl' him into the sea.

The Jonah story reminds us of Jesus and his disciples in a boat during a violent storm (Mark 4.35-41). Jesus was in a deep sleep like Jonah, but his sleep is an act of faith while Jonah's is an act of rebellion. In both cases when action is taken the tempest ceases. The sailors, just like the disciples of Jesus, are filled with awe and wonder but their response goes further! They now offer sacrifices to Yahweh (Jonah's God – the LORD) rather than to their own deities (*Elohim)*. Jonah is inadvertently leaving a trail of converts behind.

The name *Jonah ben Amittai* literally means 'dove son of faithfulness'. It conjures up a gentle creature with a homing instinct. The narrator, by including the full name is adding to the irony of the story telling. He seems to be saying to his listeners, 'Would you like to go on a relaxing ocean cruise with Jonah?'

To Ponder:
- How do you respond to the idea that a fictional story has been included in the Bible?

- What price (emotional, physical and social) do we pay for shutting ourselves away from reality?
- There are many good caring people who never go to church; some much better than those who do. How do you explain this?

2

IN THE DEPTHS OF LOCKDOWN

(17) But the Lord provided a <u>big</u> fish to swallow up Jonah; and Jonah was in the belly of the fish for three days and three nights.

(1) Then Jonah prayed to the LORD his God from the belly of the fish, (2) saying, 'I called to the LORD, out of my distress, and he answered me; out of the belly of Sheol I cried, and you heard my voice.   [Ps.18.4-6 & 120.1]

(3) You didst cast me into the deep, into the heart of the seas, and the flood surrounded me; all your waves and your billows passed over me. [Ps.42.7]

(4) Then I said, `I am driven away from your sight; how shall I again look upon your holy temple?'   [Ps.5.7]

(5) The waters closed in over me, the deep surrounded me; weeds were wrapped around my head (6) at the roots of the mountains. I went down to the land whose bars closed upon me for ever; *yet you brought my life from the Pit, O LORD my God.   [Ps.69.2 & Ps.30.3]*

(7) As my life was ebbing away, I remembered the LORD; and my prayer came to you, into your holy temple.   .[Ps.142.3 & Ps.18.5-6]

(8)Those who worship vain idols forsake their true loyalty. (9) But I with the voice of thanksgiving will sacrifice to you; what I have vowed I will pay.

Deliverance belongs to the LORD!'   [Ps.116.17-18 & Ps.3.8]

(10) Then the LORD spoke to the fish, and it spewed out Jonah upon the dry land.

For a non maritime nation like the Jews, the sea was dangerous. It symbolized the forces of chaos which, like Noah's flood, could obliterate all life. The first listeners would have asked, 'Why did Jonah attempt such a sea voyage? What was he so afraid of?' In the primal cosmic chaos of sea there lived a terrifying monster called Leviathan (Ps.74.14 & Isa.27.1). He is fully described in Job.41. He enters the Jonah story now as the 'big fish.'

In pre-modern times, readers of Jonah would have had no difficulty in believing that God could appoint a big fish to save the prophet. They would chuckle at the craziness of it. The word 'swallow' (also translated 'gulp down') would, however, wipe the smile from their faces. The Old Testament people of God would have remembered Nebuchadnezzar, king of Babylon, who like a Leviathan dragon 'devoured' ('gulped down') Israel (Jer. 51.34 & 44).

Before lockdown, 'normality' for Jonah was spent hiding from God and running away from important realities. Has this been the contemporary life-style of many people in Britain before we were hit with Covid-19? The prophet has already been in the 'belly' of the ship (1.5). Now in God's rescue plan he finds himself in the 'belly' of a fish which is the 'belly' of *Sheol* (2.2). Fact and narrative are now transposed by metaphor and image. *Sheol* is the place of death and is pictured here as a city with gates located beneath the deepest roots of the mountains.

Jonah has been trying to escape from God, but this has proved to be impossible. Psalm 139 asks,

> *'Where can I flee from your presence? If I ascend to heaven you are there; if I make my bed in Sheol, you are there... If I take the wings of the morning and settle at the farthest limits of the sea, even there your hand shall lead me' (v.7-10).*

Although *Sheol*, like a cosmic black hole', swallows everything, God is able to enter this 'underworld' to extract and save. Hosea speaks of the LORD striking us down, binding us up and raising us up 'on the third day' (6.1-2). He goes on to ask, 'O Death, where are your plagues? O *Sheol*, where is your destruction?' (13.14). Thus Paul, inspired by these words and images, will affirm that 'Death is *swallowed* up in victory' and asks, like Hosea, 'Where, O death, is thy victory? Where, O death, is thy sting? (1 Cor. 15.54).

In chapter 1, Jonah does not pray and remains tight-lipped until he is compelled to speak to the sailors. Now at rock bottom and facing certain death, prayers finally spill out. His sentences of desperation are made up of quotes from the Psalms. For hundreds of years the Psalter has been a essential resource for praying Christians. Every experience of life is recorded there: joy, pain, betrayal, hate, hope, despair, anger, anguish, praise and thanksgiving.

You will see from the references, interjected into the text above, that nearly all the words of Jonah's prayer are taken from the

Psalms. Only in verse 5 & 6 (not in italics) is there language unique to Jonah who is being smothered and drowned in a watery grave. Helplessly, entangled and enmeshed in seaweed 'the prison doors' close behind him. Note the repetition of 'deep, deep, down' (v.3, 5, 6) as Jonah goes under. On the cross in his own extremity Jesus, like Jonah, draws his prayers from the Psalms (Ps.22.1, 31.5).

In the Psalter there are two classified forms of prayer: 'lament' and 'thanksgiving'. Given the drowning experience of Jonah, we would expect this to be a 'lament'. Instead scholars have labelled it a 'Thanksgiving Psalm'. Jonah goes down but reaching the land of the dead he 'remembers'. In this ultimate place of destruction Jonah meets with God in much the same way as Job met with God in a whirlwind. At the point of annihilation the descent of these two characters is halted. God will raise them up. Jonah's prayer ends in thanksgiving as he rejoices in his 'deliverance'. We are reminded of our Lord's triumphant shout from the cross, 'It is finished'.

Jesus refers to Jonah in Matthew 12.40. 'For as Jonah was three days and nights in the belly of the sea monster', so will the Son of Man be three days and nights in the heart of the earth'. Easter Saturday is the occasion when Jesus went searching for humanity's first parents – Adam and Eve – in order to release them and their descendents from the prison of *Sheol* (1 Peter 3.19). This cosmic act of God in Christ gives assurance and hope for all humanity. Jonah is given a foretaste of God's redemptive grace which will be universally enacted. The imagery of being plunged into the water and lifted up is signified by the sacrament of baptism in which we die and are raised to life again (1 Cor.15.4; Rom.6.3-4).

In the New Testament letter to the Philippians, scholars have identified an early Christian hymn (Phil.2.6-11). It celebrates the downward self-emptying journey of Jesus who become a human being and enters the place of annihilation for our salvation. Because of his **obedience**, God the Father raises him up to the highest place. Humiliation is followed by exaltation. Jonah is taken down to the lowest place because of **disobedience.** He does not, however, remain at the bottom but is saved by the compassionate LORD. Will Jonah grasp the truth of this?   Sadly even on his upward journey of deliverance his bigoted belligerence remains. He remembers Nineveh as the place where they 'worship vain idols' (2.8).

To Ponder:
- For both Job and Jonah, divine disclosure happens in darkness, in desolation and at the point of annihilation. It is in the darkness rather than in the sunshine that we perceive the light. What do you think?
- Look up the verses from the Psalms which make up Jonah's prayer. How have your daily devotions being shaped and deepened by your own reading and familiarity with the Psalms?
- Was lockdown good for you?

3

MISSION ACCOMPLISHED

(1) The word of the LORD came to Jonah a second time, saying, (2) 'Get up, go to Nineveh, that <u>big</u> (great) city, and proclaim to it the message that I tell you.' (3) So Jonah arose and went to Nineveh, according to the word of the LORD. Now Nineveh was an exceedingly <u>big</u> (large city), a three days' walk across. (4) Jonah began to go into the city, going a day's walk. And he cried, 'Forty days more, and Nineveh shall be overthrown!' (5) And the people of Nineveh believed God; they proclaimed a fast, and everyone, great and small, put on sackcloth.

(6) When the news reached the king of Nineveh, and he rose from his throne, removed his robe, covered himself with sackcloth, and sat in ashes. (7) Then he had a proclamation made in Nineveh: 'By the decree of the king and his nobles: No human being or animal, no herd or flock, shall taste anything. They shall not feed, nor shall they drink water. (8) Human beings and animals shall be covered with sackcloth, and they shall cry mightily to God. All shall turn from their evil ways and from the violence that is in their hands. (9) Who knows? God may relent and change his mind; he may turn from his fierce anger, so that we do not perish'.

*(10) When God saw what they did, how they turned from their
evil ways, God changed his mind about the calamity that he had
said he would bring upon them; and he did not do it.*

In his prayer Jonah promised to make sacrifices and keep his
personal vows (2.9). What vows? What sacrifices? There is no
evidence of either of these declarations being kept. In a masterstroke
of irony the fish, unlike the prophet, does exactly what God tells him
to do and spits out Jonah. Covered in slime and seaweed, deposited
in an undignified fashion, the prophet has to clean himself up so that
the narrator can re-start the story.

Literary experts have shown that the theme of dying and
rising can be presented through the use of certain phrases: 'go down'
and 'rise up' or 'arise'. The phrase 'to go down' (1.3, 1.5, and 2.6)
has been used hitherto and culminates in Jonah's descent to *Sheol*.
We have already encountered the resurrection word 'arise' (1.1, 1.6).
It is now reiterated and reinforced. Moreover, as we shall see, the
king of Nineveh (3.6), on hearing God's message also 'rises up' from
his throne as a result of Jonah's mission.

Many people think of a missionary as a person who takes
God to the people. This is incorrect. We do not take God; he is there
already. The LORD of surprise seeks to physically remove us from
our comfortable place 'at home' and put us in an unfamiliar location
so that we can discover that God is already present. Peter learnt this
when he stayed at Joppa (Acts 10). Did Jonah, when he left Joppa,
recognise God's presence in the storm and in the compassionate
behaviour of the sailors? Jonah did find and acknowledge the
presence of God in the belly of the fish. Will he be shocked to
discover that this same God is already present in Nineveh? Is he

learning through these painful experiences that you cannot escape from the LORD; indeed God both pursues us and goes before us!

Jonah has literally been to hell and back. He no longer wishes to repeat the experience. So for a second time when instructed to 'arise and go', he decides to obey. The Hebrew word used for 'go' is literally an instruction to 'walk'. He has to undertake a 900 mile journey on foot following trade routes across the desert. Plenty of time to think!   What is going to happen next?   This footsore disgruntled traveller, on catching his first glimpse of the city, is overcome with dismay. The job from the start was distasteful; he now sees it to be impossible.

Nineveh was regarded with loathing by Jonah and his contemporaries (2 Kings 14.25f). The Assyrians were the Nazi storm-troopers of the ancient world – a pitiless power-crazed enemy. The prophet Nahum directs a furious blast of hate against the city. 'I will throw filth at you and treat you with contempt and make you a spectacle' (3.6). Denouncing this city would have guaranteed Jonah's popularity amongst his own people; Jonah should have rejoiced, like Nahum, at being sent as a herald of destruction. So why did he not relish this commission?

It has been suggested that Jonah, like the book of Ruth, was a religious tract written **after** the exile when, in the time of Ezra and Nehemiah, Jewish exclusivism was rampant. These two tiny books of Ruth and Jonah, with their universal message of love, acted as a prophetic blast against the religious racism of their day. The mention of Nineveh, however, suggests a date **before** the exile.

Archaeological surveys have shown Nineveh to be a vast suburban sprawl with a circumference of around sixty miles. The walled city proper with its gardens and palaces would be at the centre. It was larger than modern Mosul which adjoins the ancient site. The Bible describes it as an 'exceedingly large' metropolis 'three days walk in breadth' with a population of more than 120,000 people plus animals (4.11).

As mentioned at the beginning of chapter 2, for a non-maritime nation like the Jews, the sea was dangerous. Indeed, the Jews as a land-locked people had an inherent fear of all things aquatic. When it came to the gods of the other nations, there were a plethora of 'fish gods'. While the Philistines and the Canaanites had *Dagon* and the Egyptians had *Latos;* the Assyrians had *Nina*: the fish goddess. Nineveh, founded by King Nin-us, was thought of by the Hebrews as the '*City of Fish*'. This puts the Jonah narrative into a very fishy context. Jonah is swallowed by a big fish; Nineveh is 'big fish city'. Jonah has been in the belly of the fish for three days; the journey across Nineveh takes three days. Jonah almost died in the belly of the fish, will he again be swallowed up in Nineveh? Two repulsive experiences! Previously he prayed in desperation. Here he will preach in exasperation.

On entering the city he makes a start by shouting, 'Forty days and Nineveh shall be overthrown'. This is not exactly what God had told him to say. For Jonah the word 'overthrown' meant obliteration but did the story teller have another interpretation in mind? God could decide to 'overthrow' his destructive decree and save the city (Deu.23.5). After one day of preaching, the prophet had still not reached the city centre. His message, however, was having an immediate effect. It spread like wild-fire in a populist movement even reaching the palaces. On hearing the news, the king 'rises' from his throne, discards his garments and 'sits' in the ashes of repentance. Furthermore it is the king who reinterprets Jonah's message as the possibility of deliverance and not as a proclamation of destruction.

As with the sailors, we have another example of a pagan outsider acting with a degree of integrity and openness not found in this ridiculous prophet. In Matthew 12.39-42, Jesus spoke to his narrow minded critics of the 'sign of Jonah' in exhorting them to repent like the people of Nineveh. This same message is repeated in Matt.16.4 and Luke 11.29-32.

The king, who sits in ashes and reminds us of Job, shows remarkable insight. He recognises how violence is endemic within the whole Assyrian culture. He also has an ecological awareness of the interrelatedness of humanity and animals; something Jonah has to learn. He believes that the *Nina* fish-God could 'change her mind' because the whole city has gone into a lockdown of repentance. Unlike the sailors, however, there is no conversion to 'the LORD'.

Is the LORD actually changing his mind in this story? Although there are references to God 'repenting' in Gen.6.7, Ex 32.14, 1 Sam.15.11, the LORD does not repent. We have to repent because of our sin, but God does not sin. Divine repentance in the Old Testament usually describes God acting in a manner not anticipated. God's ways are the ways of love and are therefore not fixed within some concrete cosmic plan. God is always seeking, because of his compassion and righteousness, to redeem each and every event. As we saw, at the end of our study of Job (40.8), sometimes our prayers can actually persuade God to do things differently (Gen.18.20-33).

To Ponder:

- Does God change his mind?
- What might God be telling us to do about Putin and Russia?
- What have you learnt so far from your study of Jonah?
- 'Without God we cannot. Without us God will not.' Discuss.

4

A MIXED UP MISSIONARY

(1) But this displeased Jonah <u>*with a great displeasure*</u>*, and he became angry. (2) He prayed to the LORD and said, 'O LORD! Is not this what I said while I was still in my country? That is why I fled to Tarshish at the beginning; for I knew that you were a gracious God and merciful, slow to anger, and abounding in steadfast love, and ready to relent from punishing. (3) And now, O LORD, please take my life from me, for it is better for me to die than to live.' (4) And the LORD said, 'Is it right for you to be angry?'*

(5) Then Jonah went out of the city and sat down east of the city, and made a booth for himself there. He sat under it in the shade, waiting to see what would become of the city. (6) The LORD God appointed a bush, and made it come up over Jonah, to give shade over his head, to save him from his discomfort; so Jonah was happy <u>*with a great happiness*</u> *about the bush. (7)] But when dawn came up the next day, God appointed a worm that attacked the bush, so that it withered. (8) When the sun rose, God prepared a sultry east wind, and the sun beat down on the head of Jonah so that he was faint and asked that he might die.*
He said, 'It is better for me to die than to live.'

(9) But God said to Jonah, 'Is it right for you to be angry about the bush?' And he said, 'Yes angry enough to die.' (10) Then the

LORD said, 'You are concerned about the bush, for which you did not labour and which you did not grow; it came into being in a night and perished in a night. (11) And should I not be concerned about Nin'eveh, that great city, in which there are more than a hundred and twenty thousand people who do not know their right hand from their left, and also many animals?'

Walt Disney gave us Pinocchio. Herman Melville gave us Moby Dick. The Old Testament gives us Jonah who, a bit like Pinocchio, has to be taught a lesson. Although there is humour in this absurd story, there is little to laugh about. Jonah is as obsessed as Captain Ahab but not with the whale but with his own particular brand of religion. A thoroughly disgusted Jonah quits the city, goes outside, builds a shelter and watches. Surely fire will come down to consume this wicked monstrosity of a place? Instead God allows the city to look after itself; his attention is fixed on Jonah who sits comfortably and waits to see the end of the city. Contrast this with the pagan king who 'arose from his throne' to sit hopefully in chafing sackcloth and gritty ashes.

The narrator hasn't fully informed us of why Jonah refused his commission. Now at last the truth is out. Jonah had known from the beginning that the LORD is a gracious and loving God. The very thought that the inhabitants of Nineveh could be saved rather than slaughtered was abhorrent to him.

The narrator has kept us in suspense throughout this crazy story. His narration is dramatic, colourful and poetically shaped. For example, the end exactly balances the beginning with Jonah's speech in chapter 4 mirroring chapter 1. Both speeches are made up of exactly 39 Hebrew words. There are also parallel confessions of faith.

> I *am a Hebrew.*
> *I worship the LORD, the God of heaven,*
> *who made the sea and the dry land' (1.9).*

> *I know that you are a gracious God and merciful,*
> *slow to anger, and abounding in steadfast love,*
> *and ready to relent from punishing (4.2).*

Jonah's confession of faith shows us that he does believe that the LORD is not only the Creator but the Saviour. The word *steadfast love* is used with reference to God's love for Israel within the covenant. It is a favourite word for Hosea; something Jonah would have understood given that Hosea may have been a contemporary. But there is further irony. Job, who not being a Hebrew, has to learn about the power and providence of God; Jonah knows this already. Furthermore, Job is given examples of God's cosmological, ecological and zoological power. Jonah personally experiences these dimensions – and more – in his flight from the truth but refuses to read the signs. He has been pursued by storm, wave and fish; now he will be maligned by wind, plant and worm. The dichotomy between Jonah's verbal expression of faith and his inner spirituality is emphasised by the narrator. God is slow to anger; Jonah is not only quick to anger but nurses his anger.

The narrator saturates his story with biological, meteorological, zoological and aquatic references. He reminds us that God loves animals and doesn't want to see them destroyed. The narrator's final joke is to tell his audience that the hated king of Nineveh also shares God's concern for animals, herds and flocks, and in order to save them gives orders that they be dressed in sackcloth.

This concluding chapter is full of heat. The Hebrew word 'anger' literally translates 'burnt up' (Gen.44.18). The sun beats down on Jonah's head. Scorching blasts of wind and sand shrivel his self-esteem. The narrator emphasises Jonah's rage. Furious with God, Jonah is burnt up – inside and out. Circumstances again drive him to pray but not as he did in chapter 2. His prayer, this time around, is not shaped or inspired by the Psalms; it is a dismal moaning rant. He has had enough and wants to die.

Elijah, after the Mount Carmel incident, confesses that he too has had enough. (Look back at my sermon in Part 1). Elijah's request arises from a sense of personal failure. Jonah, on the other hand, has been successful. His prayer is motivated by self-destructive egotism. Note the repeated use of 'I', 'my' and 'me' in verses 2-3. Job had also fallen out with God. After 40 chapters of argument he finally acknowledges the wisdom and wonder of God and repents 'of dust and ashes' (42.6). There is no such outcome for Jonah. His intransigence remains. He would not be able to sing:

> *For the love of God is broader*
> *Than the measures of the mind;*
> *And the heart of the Eternal*
> *Is most wonderfully kind.*

Jonah, sitting outside the city, mopes and sulks. The shelter he built for himself is described as a 'booth'. Such shelters were built when the Feast of Tabernacles was celebrated. The feast and associate activities were to be reminders of the time Israel spent in the wilderness on their journey of salvation from Egypt to the

Promised Land. Does this suggest that Jonah is also on a journey of salvation? Like the escaping children of Israel he has passed through the waters and travelled across a desert. He has personally experienced God's salvation and acknowledges that God is merciful and kind. A new future is possible, but he will not let go and so cannot move towards it. What is God to do?

God has appointed a fish now he appoints a 'plant'. Next day he will appoint 'a worm' and then an 'east wind'. We have already encountered the 'big wind' in chapter 1. The Hebrew word for 'wind' is '*ruach*'. It is also the word for 'breath' or 'spirit' which in the New Testament is '*pneuma*'. This is the wind which blew across a desert valley of burnt up bones in Ezekiel 37.9f causing them to 'arise'. This wind later filled the apostles on the day of Pentecost (Acts 2.2). God continues to breathe life into his created world so that the plants and animals have a revelatory and renewing role. This is something Christine, in her letters mentions

First God appoints a **bush**. Jonah certainly appreciates it. He had a 'big displeasure' at the start but now he 'rejoices with a big joy' (v.6). There is an additional play on words because, in Hebrew, the 'shade' is to help Jonah 'shed' his anger. Surely at last he will renounce his fury and rejoice in God's loving kindness? He does not! Being extra kind to Jonah does not work.

Next comes a **worm**. This tiny creature destroys the bush and nibbles away at Jonah's fleeting moments of pleasure. As the sun rises a sirocco wind blasts across the desert spattering the pathetic prophet with burning sand. He now feels even sorrier for himself than before. It is the second time the prophet has experienced the wind of judgment. This also fails to bring him to his senses.

Next God tried **argument** – a 'how much more' argument (Matt.6.30, Luke 12.24, Romans 5.15). 'How can you pity the destruction of one plant yet fail to pity the destruction of 120,000 people?' The Hebrew word 'pity' or 'concern' literally means 'to have tears in your eyes'. This final question is not primarily addressed to Jonah but to the Old Testament people of God and to us. The book ends with this unsettling question. It is never answered.

So we leave the prophet sitting, sulking and snarling at the saved city. Over and against this I set the picture of Jesus gazing at Jerusalem with tears in his eyes weeping because it seems to be inhabited by a host of Jonahs (Lk.19.41-44). We, who have travelled in and out of lockdown, are now being asked, as Jonah was, whether our personal worldview has expanded or contracted and whether our compassion for others has grown or atrophied. Thomas Carlisle's poem *You Jonah* closes with these lines:

> *And Jonah stalked*
> *To his shaded seat*
> *And waited for God*
> *To come around*
> *To his way of thinking.*
> *And God is still waiting for a host of Jonahs*
> *In their comfortable houses*
> *to come around*
> *to his way of loving.*[18]

To Ponder:
- The narrator has set out Jonah's creed. Write you own creed using your own words: 'I worship the LORD.......'.   How good are you at living out your creed?

104

- Has your worldview expanded or contracted because of lockdown?
- Has post-lockdown Britain become inhabited by a host of Jonahs?

EPILOGUE

Job is commanded by God to observe the stars above and the creatures below so as to regain a sense of his true place in the order of things. Jesus tells us to look at the flowers of the field and pay close attention to the birds of the air (p.22). Plants, trees, physical places, the sea and the changing conditions of the weather figure largely in Christine's letters. All planetary life is our mission context.

That context starts with Adam and Eve surrounded by plants, fruit bearing trees, insects, birds and animals at play. Through disobedience this paradise of presence became a place of absence. Nevertheless gardens, rather than buildings continue to be key locations for the outworking of God's big story. Jesus draws attention to them and is betrayed in a garden. When this world of economics, religion and power edged Jesus out, he chose to return as a resurrection gardener. In a vision of the future, the last book of the Bible paints a picture of a garden city with no waters of chaos, no temple building, no scorching sun, no beguiling moon, no death and no curse.[19] All who thirst are invited to drink freely from the water of life flowing from the throne of God and to bask under the tree of life (Rev.22). These images keep planetary life and the challenge of climate change at the top of our mission agenda.

In the book of Jonah, the prophet is made all too aware of this ecological context as God tries to speak to him though a raging sea, violent winds, a storm, a fish, animals, a plant, the burning sun and a ravenous worm. These events however fail to dent his egocentricity. Elijah, although subjected to powerful natural phenomena including a cosmic silence, soon forgets God's lesson (p.29). Neither prophet inspires us with hope. They have received amazing revelatory disclosures through nature during their lockdowns but seem unable to break free from former patterns of thinking and behaviour. Of course, they are Old Testament figures. They lack the fullness of revelation in Christ. Like Joseph (p.10), they are players in a bigger story yet seem to be unaware of it. This story describes how we have been given responsibility to care for each other, to respect life in all its forms and to protect rather than damage our natural environment. The amazing thing is that God continues to believe in us regardless of our shortcomings. This is our story and this is our mission.

George Steiner, the extraordinary literary critic, philosopher and polymath, in one of his conversations comments on the book of Jonah. He smiles at the way in which irony is used to turn Jonah's tragic story into a comedy. Nevertheless, he finds it to be no laughing matter because it describes 'the egomania of the human intellect'.[20] In a reflection, prior to his death, he speaks of how Europe and the Western World no longer have a creative model for tomorrow. The weight of the past is too strong and robs us of the future. 'We have lived too long in an 'upside-down pyramid'.[21]

Does this mean that our Western world, in Richard Holloway's phrase, 'is waiting for the last bus?' (p.16). Have we become so self-absorbed, like Jonah, that we have lost the ability to transcend the old? Can there really be a 'new normal' or will our future be just more and more of the same within the 'old normal'? If we inhabitants of the planet, whether Christians or not, are to regain hope 'we must keep going; we are guests of life and must continue to struggle, to try to improve things, even a little.' Steiner thinks we are living in a *Long Saturday* and asks, 'Will humankind experience a Sunday?'[22] He leaves us with that question.

As Christians we do anticipate a Sunday because the resurrection of Jesus Christ, in a garden, heralds the transfiguration of the physical! We must rediscover the desolation of the cross if we are to anticipate God's new creation.[23] Like those travellers on the Emmaus Road (Lk.24) we must honestly confess our true position. 'We had hoped!' Although our present scenario is grim and the future of humanity uncertain; we are not without hope. Tiny seeds of resurrection are already present. Some of us discovered them in lockdown. These fragments of hope are scattered throughout this book:

'A pruning and an emptying process has taken place. A Holy Spirit filling is required' (p.21).

'Julian of Norwich lived through the fears of the Black Death. She held onto three truths revealed to her: God made us; God loves us: God sustains us' (p.32).

'Goodness is stronger than evil; love is stronger than hate; light is stronger than darkness; life is stronger than death; victory is ours through him who loves us' (p.38).

'After the long nasty book of Judges comes the beautiful miniscule book of Ruth. It's about how one gracious act can plant seeds of hope for future generations' (p.42).

Epilogue and Appendix

'We must keep physically connecting ourselves with the healing spirit which permeates the natural world of trees, rocks and plants' (p.72).

'We all need to find our special place where the spirit world breaks through into our earthly existence' (p.75).

'In the ministry of Jesus we also discover that 'outsiders' are often more open to compassion and truth than 'the religious insiders' (p.86).

'Sometimes our prayers can actually persuade God to do things differently' (p.97).

APPENDIX

NOTES AND REFERENCES

1. The 'I' Newspaper, 23April 2022.

2. Stuckey, *Covid-19 God's Wake-Up Call? Angry Biblical Reflections in a Pandemic*, 2021, Amazon.

3. The designation 'Chair of District', used by the Methodist Church in Britain is an equivalent Diocesan Bishop.

4. This sermon was first delivered 'on line', in September 2021, to a gathering of Methodist Ministers in Liverpool. It was remodelled in March 2022 for when I preached, for the last time, at the Southampton District Synod of which I was Chair of the District between 1998 -2005.

5. Jonathan Sacks, *Judaism's Life-Changing Ideas*, Maggid, OUPRESS, 2020, p.54.

6. Richard Holloway, *Waiting for the Last Bus: Reflections on Life and Death*, Canongate, 2019, p.155.

7. Jonathan Sacks, *Morality: Restoring the Common Good in Divided Times*, H&S, 2020.

8. John Stott, *Christian Counter-Culture: The Message of the Sermon on the Mount*, IVP, 1979. p.164.

9. Alan Lewis, *Between Cross & Resurrection: A Theology of Holy Saturday*, Eerdmans, Grand Rapids, 2001, p.463.

10. Gerald Janzen, *Job, Interpretation: A Bible Commentary for Teaching and Preaching*, John Knox, 1985; Norman Habel, *The Book of Job*,

Cambridge University Press, 2016; Gustavo Gutierrez, *Job: God-Talk and the Suffering of the Innocent,* Orbis, 1992.

11. Stuckey, ibid. p.79.

12. Tom Wright, *God and the Pandemic,* 2020 & John Lennox, *Where is God in a Coronavirus World?*

13. Stuckey, ibid. p.12.

14. Sacks, *Judaism's Life-Changing Ideas,* ibid. p.7.

15. Gustavo Gutierrez, ibid. p.102.

16. Janzen, ibid. p.252f.

17. James Limburg, *Hosea-Micah,* Interpretation, WJK, 2011, pp.137-157; Rosemary Nixon, *The Message of Jonah,* Nottingham, IVP 2003; Joyce Baldwin, 'Jonah' in T.E.McComiskey (ed.), *The Minor Prophets: Volume 2,* Grand Rapids MI: Baker Books, 1993, pp.543-590; Eugene Peterson, *Under the Unpredictable Plant,* Grand Rapids, MI, Eerdmans, 1993.

18. Thomas Carlisle's poem *You Jonah* found in J. Verkuyl, *Contemporary Missiology,* Eerdmans, 1978, p.100.

19. Joanne Cox-Darling, *Finding God in a Culture of Fear,* BRF, 2019, p.66.

20. George Steiner with Laure Adler, *A Long Saturday: Conversations,* University of Chicago Press, 2017, p.64.

21. Steiner, ibid. p.23.

22. ibid. p.24.

23. Tom Stuckey, *The Wrath of God Satisfied: Atonement in an Age of Violence*, WIPF & STOCK, Oregon, 2012.

Printed by Amazon Italia Logistica S.r.l.
Torrazza Piemonte (TO), Italy

41384986R00069